En

When it comes to setting out clear foundational values for a solid and productive Christian life, no one has more credibility than a long-time successful pastor. In *Essentials*, Pastor John Morgan gently walks us through the steps needed to have a Biblically-based worldview that will stand regardless of the challenges we may face as believers. Not only does he provide Scriptural basis for his guidance, Pastor Morgan's stories and delivery keeps you looking forward to the next steps you should take to be assured that you have all the "essentials" needed to survive whatever challenge life may throw at you. His admonition that if something is important, we find a way to do it (or if not, we find an excuse) is an incentive to be sure we have the essentials in our life to make it, regardless of the storms we might face. In *Essentials*, Pastor Morgan has created an intriguing guide for us to be confident we have the proper Scriptural foundation needed to thrive.

Arthur D. (Art) Rhodes
President/CEO
Church of God Benefits Board

In a world of aimless walkers, wishers, and workers, it is good to know that there is a "True North." Pastor John Morgan masterfully reminds of the simplicity and security of walking by faith. *Essentials* proves the Gospel is the only thing that can withstand the test of time and trials. You will be gently reminded and encouraged to run on.

Bishop Anthony Pelt
State Administrative Bishop
Church of God, Florida-Cocoa

Through *Essentials*, Pastor John V. Morgan has drawn on 30-plus years of pastoring and a lifetime of ministry to provide a guidebook of how to thrive when others are just trying to survive. His blueprints are drawn from the one book that has lasted through the test of time: the Word of God. The 10 points of focus that Pastor Morgan breaks down are a must-read for every pastor, lay leader, and Christian in the church today who desire a sustaining faith that defies all circumstances. I've known Pastor Morgan and Betsy for many years. They are a gift to the Church of God and a treasure to the Kingdom. He has helped usher the church through these troubling times. Now, let him prepare you for the next storm because, as *Essentials* reminds us, another storm is always coming.

Bishop John D. Childers
Assistant Director
Church of God World Missions

What constitutes a true disciple of Jesus? This is the question John Morgan addresses with clarity and anointing in the pages of this book. I found myself enjoying a personal revival as I read the words of this beloved pastor. With wisdom from both experience and study, John weaves a hopeful, powerful, and challenging call to follow Jesus in word and practice. *Essentials* is a book desperately needed for life in an ever-changing world like ours.

Brenda C. Pac, D.Min.
Coordinator, Community Service Chaplains
Church of God Chaplains Commission

I've known Pastor John Morgan for over three decades. Ever since we both pastored in Southwest Florida—John in Naples and me in Lehigh Acres. Within the span of 30 years you get to know and understand a few things about a person. While reading *Essentials* you'll notice them too. First, John *thinks deeply* about things, especially about things that matter. Second, John *believes genuinely*, which makes him authentic, forthright, and a man with an opinion. Third, John is a gifted musician, which means he possesses all the *unique abilities* that require attention to order, detail, commitment, and excellence. Fourth, John is truly a man who *lives out Matthew 6:33*; I've seen it. Some people seek everything else before seeking God, but not John. For these reasons, John's *Essentials* are worthy of a slow and thoughtful examination. Reading his thoughts may just assist us all in rediscovering **the key** to everything.

Dr. Fred Garmon
Founder and President, Leader Labs

Essentials is a great read for anyone—especially those who feel overwhelmed or under-equipped. Author Morgan reminds us of Jesus' instructions, "Seek first the Kingdom," which is the most essential of all the essentials. This book is a joy to read, engaging from the first page forward. It is practical, encouraging, and, more importantly, equipping. Specific action steps are provided for each of the 10 essentials. It is an excellent teaching/training tool for both individuals and groups.

Dale Denham, D.Min.
President, International Schools of Leadership Development

From the wealth of experience forged over years of credible and successful ministry, within this book John Morgan takes readers on a heart-lead journey of absolutes. This is a must read for anyone who desires to live a Christ-centered life. Understand the *keys* of successful living. Learn the *Essentials*.

Dr. Stephen P. Darnell
Chancellor, European Theological Seminary
Field Director of Europe, Middle East, CIS
Church of God World Missions

ESSENTIALS

To Victoria

John Moe

Matthew 6:33

ESSENTIALS

Christian Living

IN A CHAOTIC
WORLD

JOHN V. MORGAN

Director of Publications: David W. Ray
Managing Editor of Publications: Lance Colkmire
Editorial Assistant: Elaine McDavid
Copy Editor: Esther Metaxas
Graphic and Layout Design: Stephanie Grable
Cover Design: Tina M. Richardson

ISBN: 978-1-64288-273-5

Please direct inquiries to Pathway Press, 1080 Montgomery Avenue, Cleveland, TN 37311. *www.pathwaypress.org*

DEDICATION

To the grandchildren:
Hayden, Connor, Sergio, Piper, Abram,
Julian, Ava, Cate, Henry, and Simon

With prayers that you will always be Matthew 6:33 people

CONTENTS

FOREWORD

The Church of God is replete with ministers who have proven their callings and ministries not just over time, but through the dynamic demonstrations of soul-winning, church growth, and Kingdom influence. Throughout the rich history of this movement, we have seen a reaping of the harvest through those leaders who have surrendered their lives to be anointed preachers of the Gospel and passionate pastors who shepherd their congregations with excellence and integrity.

When describing the attributes of what makes a great leader and pastor, I am drawn to the proven characteristics of my longtime colleague in ministry, Pastor John Morgan. He is one of the premier pastors in the Church of God, having invested his life into the lives of countless individuals. Standing alongside him in the journey has been his wife, Betsy, who has been a rock-steady partner in ministry, and a witness to those in his sphere of influence. She serves on the board for the Church of God Division of Care, and they both are members of numerous state boards.

John's travels to all parts of the world, including 18 countries across six continents, have equipped him with an enlarged burden for the global harvest. In addition, he is a published author with the release of *Standing at the Edge of the Water*. Pastor Morgan is also an accomplished musician and recording artist, using his God-given talents as one of the instruments in his soul-seeking toolbox.

That "toolbox" is where John Morgan receives his credentials to write *Essentials* with authority. As a fourth-generation Pentecostal and senior pastor for nearly 40 years, Pastor Morgan has the life experience to address some of the most fundamental challenges of pastoral ministry. As a church planter he has lived what it takes to dig the wells and establish the roots of a growing and thriving congregation.

His 24-year leadership of Restoration Church—a thriving body of believers in Jacksonville, Florida—has given him invaluable insights into leading a multicultural congregation.

The simplicity of the title of this book and its 10 chapters demonstrates the wisdom of Pastor Morgan as he presents the *essentials* of ministry in an easy-to-grasp style. These 10 principles, as he eloquently outlines and describes in the first chapter, are the keys to everything in ministry. Starting from the lens of every pastor's recent major ministry hurdle—the Covid-19 pandemic—Pastor John gets back to the basics that everyone called to pastoral ministry should take heed. He hits the high points, including worship, Scripture, servanthood, family, giving, and witnessing to emphasize their critical importance in an age when every ministry leader encounters the compulsion to go after "the next big thing." While that "thing" may be effective, seeking it while forsaking the essentials of ministry is a path doomed to failure.

Essentials is destined to become a volume of regular reference for church leaders as it goes back to the basics of ministry. These ministry basics align with the core values of the Church of God, and grasping and implementing them in ministry is both necessary and Scriptural. As a pastor, I could multiply my time by using *Essentials* as both a textbook and workbook to teach as a resource on Sunday night or in small groups. It is doctrinally sound and written in a compelling and entertaining way.

Pastors, this book is not only for you, but also for the people who you shepherd. It will serve as a divine guidebook for the ministry journey, and I highly recommend it.

Raymond F. Culpepper
First Assistant General Overseer
Church of God (Cleveland, Tennessee)

INTRODUCTION

When I announced "You've Never Been This Way Before" as the title of my New Year's message on the first Sunday of 2020, I never imagined how true, almost prophetic, it would prove to be. The beginning of 2020 was a whirlwind of activity. Soon after the hectic holiday season at the end of 2019 and the beginning of the New Year, I led a group of people from my congregation on a ten-day trip to Israel.

February began with the celebration of family birthdays, followed by meetings with an architect about a proposal to enlarge and renovate our church facilities. Throw in going on a road trip for a couple of days to a leadership meeting with ministry peers . . . playing for a hymn sing with senior adults . . . preaching a funeral . . . leading church-worship services . . . and February was history.

The last two days of February and the first of March, we held our church's annual missions conference. Immediately after the Sunday-morning missions service, I was driven to the airport to board a plane for Bulgaria, where for the next week, I preached the national conference for the Church of God in that country, as well as visiting with the overseer of the Church of God in Greece for a couple of days.

During those first months of 2020, I occasionally heard rumblings about a strange virus that had started to make its way out of China, but thought little of it. Too much was happening in ministry for me to pay much attention to the news. Plans were already being put in place for my next trip out of the country, the demands of the pastorate were always present, and the grand celebration of Easter was just a few weeks away.

The Sunday after returning from Bulgaria was church as usual. The next day, the wheels fell off. By the weekend, the directive had been issued for people to quarantine at home, businesses could not open, and churches should not congregate.

Overnight we went from full-blown services with the building filled with people to a socially distanced skeleton crew and me preaching to a camera. I quickly grew to appreciate the previous investments we had made in technology because for the next ten weeks, the only worship experiences available to us were conducted online.

Thankfully, we had already begun livestreaming our services, so we were familiar with the process. However, an online platform revealed how much we needed to upgrade and improve our presentation. Online giving was in place, so our people had the tools to continue supporting the mission and ministry of the church even when they couldn't assemble in the building, but many had not yet grown accustomed to giving in that fashion. The things we had in place put us ahead of the curve, but those first weeks were still a mad scramble of creativity and innovation as we sought to provide tools and resources that would effectively serve our people and our community during the crisis.

Overnight, we were forced to come up with new ways of connecting with our people and keeping them engaged with one another. Tension built and frustration mounted when people became ill and were admitted to the hospital, as ministers and even family members were not allowed entrance to give support, encourage, and care.

No one could tell us how long we would be out of the building, and no one could predict what things would look like when and if we returned. Once the initial wave passed, about four weeks into the lock-down, I found myself in a panic. Not because of the virus, or the reports of the devastating effects it was having in our country and around the world. I wasn't panicked because of a lack of food or other essential resources my family and I needed for survival (even though the store shelves were still ridiculously low on toilet paper for some reason).

My panic was much deeper than that. The uncertainty of how long we would be unable to meet in person as the church caused me to question whether I had done the job I needed to do as pastor to prepare people for the possibility of never again being able to assemble as the church in corporate worship. I began to play "What if?" in my mind.

What if we were unable to come together as the church again? What if we didn't have the digital means to connect? What if I were prohibited from preaching and teaching God's Word to the people? If the church was no longer available, was their spiritual foundation strong enough to keep them enduring to the end? Could they and would they be able to continue serving the Lord without the religious structures in place, or would they falter and fail? Had I, as the pastor, done my job to adequately prepare them to continue to be followers of Jesus if the church and everything connected to it were suddenly stripped away?

This book was born out of those questions. It began as a series of messages preached to the congregation I've been privileged to serve since December 1998. I preached those messages not long after we were able to assemble for in-house worship once again. They were an attempt to distill the characteristics of what constitutes a true disciple of Jesus into the essential elements. In them I attempted to answer this question: What are the distinguishing marks that separate true followers of Jesus from everybody else in the world?

This is by no means an exhaustive list. You may want to add some things I've missed and perhaps remove some things you don't feel are of primary importance.

What follows, however, is my best attempt at articulating specific characteristics that are essential marks of a true follower of Jesus. Journey with me through these pages as we strip away the excess, get back to basics, and discover what it really means to be a Christ-follower.

These are the things I have encouraged the people I serve to pursue as they seek to walk out an authentic faith in a chaotic world. If we will get these things right, I believe we will be able to endure even if the organized church we have always known is removed. Whatever else we do, we must not ignore the essentials.

1

The Key to Everything

It had been a challenging day. Two extended layovers and a most unhappy child in the seat behind me on the last flight made for a grueling journey that seemed interminable. My last exhausted thought while crawling under the covers in the hotel room was one of gratitude that I didn't have to get up early because the first session of the conference where I was speaking didn't begin until the afternoon.

Mid-morning, I was startled awake from a sound sleep by a sharp rap on the door and a voice announcing, "Housekeeping!" Before I could respond, I heard the key turn in the lock and the door opening. In my fatigue I had neglected to place the *Do Not Disturb* card on the door. The only thing barring the housekeeper's entrance and subjecting her and me to embarrassment was the small chain I had remembered to secure across the top the night before. Murmuring an apology, she quickly closed the door and I attempted to bring my heart rate back down.

The housekeeper had used a master key to gain entrance to my room. In former days, this master key was also called a *skeleton key*. With the modern electronic locks, it's usually just a card. Either way, the one who holds this key has access to any room in the hotel.

At the beginning of talking about the essentials needed to be a follower of Jesus, I want to give you a *master key*. It's the key to success, happiness, and sufficiency; to spiritual, emotional, psychological, and physical health; to satisfaction, fulfillment, and contentment. This is the master key for life, and it's found tucked away in the middle of what we commonly call the "Sermon on the Mount."

The primary message of Jesus was the Kingdom of God, and Jesus identified the principles by which His Kingdom operates in this sermon. He defined the characteristics and qualities of the person who is a citizen of His Kingdom. In the middle of this teaching on the Kingdom, Jesus put the master key to life in our hand when He said, *"But seek first His kingdom and His righteousness, and all these things will be added to you"* (Matthew 6:33).

You don't have to be a Bible scholar to realize we live in a time of great uncertainty. People are fearful and anxious. If you allow yourself to focus on all the unknowns in our world right now, it's easy to give in to worry.

Even followers of Jesus seem to be better at worrying than they are at resting. Worry is excessive concern over the affairs of life. It's an all-consuming feeling of uncertainty and fear. One of the greatest challenges we face is how to handle the worry that intrudes into our lives. A lot of sleep is lost because of worry. Relationships are strained to the breaking point because of worry. Creative energy is destroyed because of worry. Many physical ailments could be eliminated if we could just figure out how to manage the worry.

In the Sermon on the Mount, Jesus gives a prescription for getting off the worry-go-round. In Matthew 6:25, He starts talking about the problem of worry and illuminates three truths about worry.

Worry Is Irreverent

Worry displaces God in your life. When you worry, you leave God out of the picture, living as though He doesn't exist. When you worry, you live as though you alone can solve your problems. Worry fails to believe God is in control. Worry fails to believe the same God who gave life is also capable of sustaining it.

It reminds me of Larry Henshaw, who wrote about the time his home was rocked by an earthquake. His young daughters,

Debbie and Carol, were locked in their bedroom when the earthquake caused their beds to slide across the room in front of the door. They panicked and began to scream for help, but Dad couldn't get in because the door was blocked by the beds.

So, Larry came to the door of the bedroom and began to speak very calmly to his girls. He told them, "Don't worry, girls! You're Henshaws . . . and Henshaws know how to keep cool heads in a crisis." There was a pause on the other side of the door. Then he heard Carol's little voice as she tearfully said, "Daddy, I think we take after Mommy's side of the family!"

Isn't that the problem with most of us? We take after the fleshly side of the family and forget about the relationship we have with our loving heavenly Father. Crisis may indeed come, but we should never lose sight of Matthew 6:30:

> If God gives such attention to the appearance of wild-flowers—most of which are never even seen—don't you think He'll attend to you, take pride in you, do His best for you? (MSG).

Worry Is Irrelevant

Worry all you want—it isn't going to change anything. That's why Jesus said, *"And who of you by being worried can add a single hour to his life?"* (v. 27).

At the end of the day, worry is futile. Worry short-circuits the processes needed to be able to find proper solutions to problems. It robs creative energy. Most of the things you worry about never happen. Worry even compounds the problem by creating stress overload . . . which leads to additional worry . . . which creates more stress . . . and it becomes a never-ending cycle of destruction.

Why don't you stop just a moment and tap yourself on the shoulder and tell yourself and say it out loud, "Worry is futile."

Worry Is Irresponsible

Worry distracts us from the things that really matter in life. It burns up energy that should be used constructively to address the problem. Jesus said worry cannot add anything to your life, and research tells us it may shorten it. Nothing is fixed by worry. Nothing is helped by worry. That's why Jesus said:

> Give your entire attention to what God is doing right now, and don't get worked up about what may or may not happen tomorrow. God will help you deal with whatever hard things come up when the time comes (v. 34 MSG).

I've discovered it isn't difficult to define the problem of worry, and it's easy to dismiss the problem of worry by telling people not to do it. The challenge is in developing the strategy and the protocol to get out of the worry. This is where we need the master key.

After talking about the problem of worry, Jesus identified the key to not only conquer the worry, but to all of life as well. It's called priority, and it's found in verse 33: *"But seek first His kingdom and His righteousness, and all these things will be added to you."*

To *seek* is to look for . . . to go in search of . . . to request. To *seek* is to pursue diligently. When you survey the landscape of your life, what are your top priorities? If you're unsure where to begin, start with your calendar and your money. Time (your calendar) is life, and your bank account represents the time it takes to make the money. Once you identify where you spend the bulk of your time and money, you'll have identified your priorities.

The problem isn't that we lack time to pursue the Kingdom. After all, we watch TV . . . we post on social media. We don't fail to pursue the Kingdom because of a lack of energy. We find enough energy to play golf, go fishing, or pursue other recreational hobbies. Not pursuing the Kingdom isn't because of a lack of money—we have a car and a smartphone. Our real problem has to do with priorities—what's important to us. The root word of *priority* is *prior*. This is what comes before anything else—what takes precedence. *Priority* refers to what occupies first place; what is before anything and everything else.

The German writer Johann Wolfgang von Goethe grasped the importance of priorities. He said, "Things which matter most must never be at the mercy of things which matter least." I've discovered if something is important to me, I'll find a way. If not, I'll find an excuse.

Jesus said the master key to everything is priority—seek *first*. There are two priority options or directions on which you can focus your life. You can go after and be occupied with things as your goal, or you can seek first the Kingdom and righteousness of God as your goal.

Most of us live life **our** way. We give **ourselves** first priority. As a result, we go after the material things that loom large in life and give small attention to the spiritual things. Most of the things we devote time, energy, and resources to are selfish—things that revolve around me, my, and mine—often ignoring the spiritual things of eternal value as if they will somehow take care of themselves.

As long as our focus is on the temporal, there are going to be a lot of reasons to worry. We'll worry about the checking account being overdrawn and not having enough to pay the bills. We'll worry about getting a job; or if we have a job, we'll worry if it's going to last, or if we'll get the promotion. We'll worry about finding the right person to marry. We'll worry about having children, and when we have them then they will give us a whole new set of things to worry about!

We'll worry about family relationships turning sour. We'll worry about our health. We'll worry about success, satisfaction, sufficiency, and security.

Jesus never denies the concerns of this life. He affirms the heavenly Father knows we need food, drink, clothing, security, and sufficiency. Rather than obsessing about those things, He admonishes us to put those concerns in the Father's hands. Trust Him with the cares of this life, and focus on the Kingdom. It seems counterintuitive, but the less we worry about the necessities of life and focus on pursuing the Kingdom, the easier life becomes.

Seek the Kingdom

The Kingdom of God is that which recognizes and promotes His rule and reign. To seek first God's Kingdom is to seek first His rule, His will, and His authority. Seeking God's Kingdom is losing yourself in obedience to Him. To seek first His Kingdom is to pour out your life into the eternal work of the heavenly Father. It's a single-minded focus that says, "I want Jesus as Lord in my life. I want to know and please Him more than anything else."

Romans 14:17 gives insight about the nature of the Kingdom: *"For the Kingdom of God is not a matter of what we eat or drink, but of living a life of goodness and peace and joy in the Holy Spirit"* (NLT).

An Old Testament prophet knew something about this Kingdom when he wrote:

> He has told you, O man, what is good; and what does the Lord require of you but to do justice, to love kindness, and to walk humbly with your God? (Micah 6:8).

The values of the Kingdom are given in Zechariah 7:9-10:

> This is what the Lord of Heaven's Armies says: "Judge fairly, and show mercy and kindness to one another. Do not oppress widows, orphans, foreigners, and the poor. And do not scheme against each other" (NLT).

Seeking first the Kingdom means to get into God's Word and find out what He wants to see in your life. Invest your time, energy, and resources in things of eternal value. Put God and the things of God first. Commit to pursuing His goal for your life with all your strength.

I've discovered the best way to find happiness is to stop seeking happiness and start seeking to please the Lord, who is the giver of real joy. The best way to experience health is to stop seeking health and seek the Healer. The best way to gain more time is not to seek better time management but cultivate a relationship with the One who is the beginning of time. The best way to receive a miracle isn't to seek for a miracle, but to seek the Miracle Worker.

Seek His Righteousness

Righteousness begins with faith and trust in Jesus. It comes as a work of divine grace when you surrender to Jesus, and He then imputes to you His righteousness. It is sustained as you pursue the character of godliness; as you seek to live, think, talk, and be like Jesus. Righteousness is lived out as you obey the word of the Lord; as you surrender to the will of the Lord; as you follow the way of the Lord.

Satisfaction, security, and supply all come as we seek first the Kingdom of God and His righteousness. In Colossians 3:2, the Apostle Paul said, *"Set your mind on the things above, not on the things that are on earth."*

This is the Master Key—priorities! We must seek the Kingdom of God and His righteousness first.

The Sermon on the Mount identifies the *problem*, gives instruction about *priority*, and then illustrates the *promise*. It's at the end of verse 33: *"all these things will be added to you."*

All we need isn't found in career, relationship, recreation, or any of the multitudes of other pursuits of this world. All we need is found in a Person—Jesus.

Apparently, there are two ways of getting *things*. We can make them the object of life and struggle for them like the world does, or we can have them added to us. Jesus says that if we seek first the Kingdom, then we can leave the secondary matters to His providential care. If God's priorities become our priorities, He promises He will take care of our needs.

When we seek first His Kingdom and His righteousness, the first thing we are promised is His **divine presence**. This is God's promise in Jeremiah 29:13: *"You will seek Me and find Me when you search for Me with all your heart."* It's also the promise of Proverbs 18:24: *"There is a friend who sticks closer than a brother."*

In Isaiah 43:2-3, God promised:

> "When you're in over your head, I'll be there with you.
> When you're in rough waters, you will not go down.
> When you're between a rock and a hard place, it won't
> be a dead end—because I am God, your personal God,
> The Holy of Israel, your Savior" (MSG).

This is the promise of Hebrews 13:5: *"He Himself has said, 'I will never desert you, nor will I ever forsake you.'"*

"All these things" means divine presence. It also means **divine provision**. In Matthew 6:26, Jesus said:

> "Look at the birds, free and unfettered, not tied down to
> a job description, careless in the care of God. And you
> count far more to him than birds" (MSG).

It's the promise of divine provision. The king-psalmist David wrote, *"I have been young and now I am old, yet I have not seen the righteous forsaken, or his descendants begging bread"* (Psalm 37:25).

His promise is Philippians 4:19: *"And my God will supply all your needs according to His riches in glory in Christ Jesus."*

His promise is 2 Corinthians 9:10-11:

> For God is the one who provides seed for the farmer
> and then bread to eat. In the same way, he will provide
> and increase your resources and then produce a great
> harvest of generosity in you. Yes, you will be enriched
> in every way so that you can always be generous (NLT).

When you seek first His Kingdom and His righteousness, He'll make sure you have all the provision you need for this life and the next.

Life can go in one of two directions, but it cannot go in both. Life cannot have a divided focus. We can live for ourselves or we can live for Jesus; we cannot live for both.

The master key—the key to a fulfilled, abundant life—is priorities: *Seek first His kingdom and His righteousness and all these things will be added unto you.*

2

Passionately Committed

W e have a problem. It isn't a pandemic problem, or an economic problem, or a social-injustice problem, or a racial problem. The late Vance Havner defined the problem of this age by saying, "There is *anarchy* in the world, there is *apostasy* in the church, and there is *apathy* in the pew."

This isn't anything new. King David spoke about the problem in Psalm 12:1-2:

> Help, O Lord, for the godly are fast disappearing! The faithful have vanished from the earth! Neighbors lie to each other speaking with flattering lips and deceitful hearts (NLT).

The prophet Isaiah was able to look through the telescope of time and speak to the problem of our age:

> Our courts oppose the righteous, and justice is nowhere to be found. Truth stumbles in the streets and honesty has been outlawed. Yes truth is gone, and anyone who renounces evil is attacked (Isaiah 59:14-15a NLT).

Jesus issued a warning about the problem: *"Sin will be rampant everywhere, and the love of many will grow cold"* (Matthew 24:12 NLT).

The dilemma in which we find ourselves is reminiscent of what was happening in ancient Israel when the prophet Elijah came on the scene. Years before, civil war had split the nation into the northern kingdom, known as Israel, and the southern kingdom (Judah). From its beginning, Israel had suffered a series of corrupt kings. When Elijah burst on the scene, the reigning monarch was a man named Ahab.

According to the Bible, Ahab was the evilest of all the kings to ever take the throne of Israel (1 Kings 16:33). Under Ahab, an alliance had been formed between Israel and the king of Phoenicia. That alliance was sealed with the marriage of Ahab to the Phoenician king's daughter, Jezebel.

Jezebel followed the religion of her own people, and thus was an ardent worshiper of Baal, the Canaanite god of rain, lightning, and thunder. When Jezebel moved to Israel, she brought her gods and the worship of her gods with her. Instead of denouncing that as false religion, Ahab joined her in worship and led the people of Israel to do the same.

Elijah was sent by God to call the people back to a relationship with Him. He issued a challenge to the priests of Baal and Asherah to meet him on the top of Mount Carmel for a contest to determine the true God. With King Ahab, 450 prophets of Baal and a vast throng of people spread out before him, Elijah's voice rang out over the mountain range: *"How long will you hesitate between two opinions? If the Lord is God, follow Him; but if Baal, follow him"* (1 Kings 18:21).

The people's response? Crickets. Nobody in Israel was willing to completely abandon Jehovah, including wicked King Ahab. However, these new gods had greater mass appeal. Fewer restrictions . . . less demanding . . . more accommodating…much more freedom to live the way they wanted and satisfy personal desires. The people were torn: not willing to completely commit to one over the other, pressured from both sides, and so they were silent.

Although the nation was founded on the belief in *monotheism* (belief there is only one God), by the time of Ahab and Jezebel it had become decidedly *polytheistic* (belief and worship of multiple gods).

I wonder if the same can't be said of the current state of Christianity. We proclaim a belief in one God, and we declare allegiance to Jesus, but too many of us are living polytheistic lives, which leads to this question: What is more important—what we say, or what we do?

Here's what I know. Those idols the Bible talks about—those rival gods—haven't gone away. They just look different today than they did then. They've gotten sneaky. They're more devious than ever.

An idol isn't always easily identified. It isn't always some hideous looking creature carved out of wood or fashioned from precious metal. Idolatry is when we put something at the center of our priorities, where only God belongs, to try to get something only God has the power to give. Even something good can be made into an idol when we give it our ultimate devotion; when we put it in the center where only God belongs, and we make it the priority of our life.

There's another truth about idols. Prosperity tends to hide our idols, while crisis tends to reveal our idols. In other words, as long as things are going well for us, we don't think we have an idolatry problem. But let a crisis come into our life—finances are threatened, our career is going down the tubes, a relationship hits the skids, we come down with a serious illness, or a pandemic threatens the stability of our world. Suddenly, we begin to realize we were counting on this thing for our security, and our self-image, and our satisfaction. Without it, we're at a loss.

John Calvin said, "The human heart is an idol factory." Not only do we live in a society filled with idols, but we have an idol factory in our own heart. The question isn't, do we have an idol problem? The real question is, which idol is the biggest rival to God in our life? There are a lot of options for idols in our modern world.

Money

This wannabe god is perhaps the most obvious. Money wants to be more than just a medium of exchange; it wants to take top priority in our life. Jesus warned in Luke 16:13, *"You cannot serve both God and money."*

Success

Some people build their whole lives around and sacrifice everything for success. Health is ruined, families are ignored, and lives are trashed at the altar of work and career.

Education

Ever hear somebody brag about his or her degrees or education? That can be an idol. We all want to impress with how smart we are.

Attractiveness/Appearance

This is a huge idol in our modern western world. People spend tons of money and effort and time, and even go through physical pain and surgeries, for this one.

Relationships

This one is a little more subtle. A relationship can become an idol if it's put in the wrong place. Some people are so afraid of losing a relationship or of being rejected that they wreck their lives and disobey God because the relationship seems supremely important. It's become an idol.

Pleasure

This one covers a lot of ground. Everything from drugs, to porn, to sex, to video games, to sports, to unhealthy eating habits, to shopping.

There are a lot of ways people orient their lives around self-gratification. We call it a *habit* or, in extreme cases, an *addiction*. The Bible calls it *idolatry*.

Another Idol

Undoubtedly there is another idol—one I haven't labeled—but it captures your attention. Just because I didn't name it, your first instinct is to think it's not an issue; but if you're honest, you'll recognize it as a potential idol for your life.

With those potential idols listed, now it's time to evaluate. Which one of those do you find yourself thinking about the most? Maybe when you're daydreaming or just having stray thoughts? Which one do you find yourself gravitating back to again and again?

Here are some more questions:

- Which of those do you most fear losing?
- Which one tempts you to feel like life might not be worth living if you didn't have this or if you lost it?
- Which one makes you feel that, because you are this or because you have this, you're *somebody* and makes you feel good about yourself?
- Which of them do you most depend upon to make you feel secure; but if you lost it, you'd feel insecure?
- Which of these do you most want to be known for?
- Which of them most easily causes your emotions to fluctuate—making you happiest when you have lots of it, but sad when it's threatened?
- Which of them would other people who know you well say is your most likely idol?
- Which one of those gets the largest share of your time and effort?
- Which one do you sacrifice the most for?

Everybody is tempted by some idol. So, the first step is simply recognizing which idol it is for you. Which one is the biggest competitor for God's place in your life?

You and I are going to worship something. We may not call it worship. We may not do it consciously with specific acts that we associate with worship, but we are going to worship

21

and serve someone or something. We must decide which god we're going to serve. Indecision isn't an option. Refusing to choose isn't an option. If we don't consciously make a choice, something or someone will step in and occupy the space.

A true follower of Jesus is passionately committed to Jesus. It's someone who has placed Jesus in the center of their life. It's a person whose worship is reserved for Jesus.

The message of Elijah to the polytheistic culture in which he lived is the same message the Lord wants to say to us today. It's time to stop wavering. Quit vacillating. We must make up our mind. Decide.

Here's what wavering looks like:

- God, please keep me out of hell and get me to Heaven, but I still want to do whatever I want to do.
- God, I want all of Your blessings, but I don't want to stop going my way instead of Your way.
- God, I want You to bless my finances, but I'm not going to give You the first part of my increase.
- God, please answer my prayers and bless me, but something else is going to get top priority in my life.

Here's what the Lord would say to those who are wavering. Stop being a Christian on Sunday and somebody else on Monday. Stop claiming to be a Christian if you're acting at work like you don't know Me. Stop wanting the benefits while being unwilling to sacrifice. Choose a side. Quit wavering.

If your false god is what's most important to you, then go all the way with it. Sell out to it. *If Baal is God, follow him.*

If possessions are really the most important thing, then quit being halfhearted about it. Go for it. Get into massive debt. Put all your time and effort into financial acquisition because that's your god. And don't ever give anything or do anything generous because that would be wavering. That would take away from your **worship of accumulating possessions.**

If your looks are your god, then don't just halfway do it. Buy whatever clothes you desire. Get all the right accessories and forget the cost. Get into the gym several hours a day. Who cares if you have time for anything else? Tan it, tweak it, puff it, tuck it, lift it, twist it, curl it, color it. Ignore the fact you're going to get old and die. The god of your appearance doesn't want you to think about that.

How about the god of sexual pleasure? If that's your god, go for it. Don't let something as insignificant as marriage hold you back. If you're not married, more power to you. Do whatever you want with whomever you desire. Go for it all the way.

However, if you're going to be a true follower of Jesus, you're going to be passionately committed to Him. You can't be a disciple of Jesus and have divided loyalties. If you're going to serve the Son of God, quit wavering. Serve Him with all your heart. You can't run with the devil all week and stand with Jesus on Sunday. You can't go to bed with Satan and wake up with Jesus. Don't claim to be following Jesus but then live as if He doesn't exist and as if He doesn't have a claim on your life. Serve Him all the way without reservation.

Being a follower of Jesus requires an exclusive, single-minded focus. In Luke 9:62, Jesus said, *"No one after putting his hand to the plow and looking back, is fit for the kingdom of God."*

Being a follower of Jesus requires the obedience He described in **Matthew 7:21:**

> "Knowing the correct password—saying 'Master, Master' for instance—isn't going to get you anywhere with me. What is required is serious obedience—doing what my Father wills" (MSG).

Being a follower of Jesus requires the sold-out surrender He proclaims in Matthew 16:24: *"If anyone wishes to come after Me, he must deny himself, and take up his cross and follow Me."*

When Elijah issued the challenge to those assembled on Mount Carmel, the people remained silent. So, he proposed a clinical trial, with a standardized test protocol for each side. Both Yahweh and Baal claimed to be able to control thunder, lightning, and storms. Elijah proposed an experiment to test their claims. Each side would slay a bull and lay it on an altar. The first deity to burn up the sacrifice wins.

Elijah graciously allowed the prophets of Baal first crack. They killed the bull, placed it on the altar, and called on Baal to send fire. Nothing happened. Several hours of praying and calling on Baal elapsed. Still nothing.

After they had been going at it most of the morning, Elijah started heckling them: "Hey! Maybe you should shout louder. Maybe your god's asleep. Maybe he's on a trip to Disney World and won't get back until next Thursday. Maybe he's busy in the bathroom."

Incensed, the prophets of Baal got louder and more frenzied. They screamed and danced for another three hours. They even cut themselves trying to attract Baal's attention. But the Bible says, *"There was no voice, no one answered, and no one paid attention"* (1 Kings 18:29).

Finally, it was Elijah's turn. He repaired the altar. He laid the sacrifice. He even drenched the whole thing with twelve barrels of water so the sacrifice was soaked, the wood was saturated, and even the trench dug around the base of the altar was filled. After making those preparations, he prayed a simple but sincere prayer. Then the fire of the Lord fell and consumed the burnt offering and the wood and the stones and the dust, and licked up the water that was in the trench (v. 38).

When the people saw the fire, *"they fell on their faces; and they said, 'The Lord, He is God; the Lord, He is God'"* (v. 39).

By now you may be thinking, *Well, if I could see a sign as spectacular as fire falling from the sky, then there would be no question. I'd make the choice to be passionately committed to following Jesus alone.*

The reality is that God has already sent you a sign that is way more impressive than sending fire from Heaven.

His sign is a Baby in a manger: *"And the Word became flesh, and dwelt among us, and we beheld His glory, glory as of the only begotten from the Father, full of grace and truth"* (John 1:14).

His sign is a Man on a cross: *"For God so loved the world, that He gave His only begotten Son, that whoever believes in Him shall not perish, but have eternal life"* (John 3:16).

His sign is an empty tomb: *"Christ died for our sins according to the Scriptures and that He was buried, and that He was raised on the third day according to the Scriptures"* (1 Corinthians 15:3b-4).

The Lord has already given all the signs we need in Jesus Christ:

- a virgin birth
- a virtuous life
- a vicarious suffering
- a victorious resurrection
- a visible return (which we are awaiting).

Every sign we need is contained in a person—Jesus, the Son of God.

How long will you hesitate between two opinions? If the gods of this world—the gods of success, pleasure, money, and relationships—are Lord, serve them. Serve them with abandon.

But if Jesus is Lord, then serve Him. You can't be halfhearted. You can't waver when it comes to your commitment to Jesus.

The Lord is speaking to you through Elijah, calling you to a point of decision. If you haven't yet surrendered your life to follow Jesus, He's calling you to make a choice. If you claim to be a born-again believer, He's calling you to get off the fence and fully commit.

Being a true follower of Jesus means you are passionately committed to Him. How long will you hesitate between two opinions?

3

Biblically Measured

Have you ever wondered who decided the length of an inch? Why not make it just a little longer or perhaps a bit shorter than it is on the measuring tape? Or why is the liquid that constitutes an ounce such an arbitrary amount? What about calling 440 sound vibrations per second the musical tone *A*? Why not let that be another note and adjust all the rest of the scale accordingly? Or why not set the note *A* to 430 or to 450?

Regardless of what you are measuring, the unit of measure must always be the same for the results to have any meaning. If two men were constructing a building, but their tape measures were not the same standard, the results would be disastrous. If the recipe called for a certain number of ounces, but the measuring cup of the person doing the baking was different from the person who designed the recipe, the product wouldn't be edible. When the orchestra was tuning, if some instruments tuned to A-440, others tuned to A-450, and still others tuned to A-430, the resultant discord would be most unpleasant to the ear.

If life is to function properly, each tape measure must be the same distance for an inch. Each ounce must contain the same amount of liquid. Each tuner must calibrate the vibrations accurately. Each of the measuring devices is set to a standard. If there is any variation from the standard, the result is chaos. It never works to let everybody decide on his or her own preferred measurement. For the sake of accuracy and for the sake of proper operation, there must be a standard.

The same is true when it comes to those who are followers of Jesus. There is a standard by which to measure whether someone is truly following Jesus. An essential character trait of the person who is a true follower of Jesus is his or her life is Biblically measured.

Biblically measured means you evaluate your experience by the Word of God rather than evaluating the Word by your experience. When your experience or your feelings or your understanding is at odds with the message of the Bible, you bow your knee in submission and give credence and authority to the Word above your experience, feelings, and understanding.

Hearing and Heeding

A true follower of Jesus isn't merely Word-believing but is also Word-living. The foundation on which a life of faith in Jesus is built is the Bible, the Word of God. Not just hearing, but heeding. Hearing isn't the equivalent of heeding.

Many people *hear* the Word, but it only becomes a solid foundation for life when we start to *heed* and *do* the Word. Only then can it become an agent of life transformation.

At the end of Matthew 7, Jesus wraps up His Sermon on the Mount. For three chapters He has taught how to become a citizen of the Kingdom of Heaven and defined the characteristics of those who live as citizens of that Kingdom. His teachings about lifestyle, priorities, and motivations were directly opposite to the world in which He lived, and they are still at odds with the lifestyle, priorities, and motivations of the world in which we live.

In concluding His teaching, Jesus finished with an illustration about two men. One is wise; the other, foolish. On the surface there doesn't seem to be a lot of difference between them. Both men are in construction, industriously building a house—we might speak of it as a life. Both are diligent, meticulous, careful—giving attention to detail.

The houses they build are remarkably similar. About the same square footage. Same features. Same quality of workmanship. They both might become showplaces in a parade of homes. When the certificate of occupancy is issued, each builder looks back on the life he has built for himself with satisfaction. It looks good. It's comfortable. It's according to plan. It's a dream come true.

There is something else these two men have in common—they both go through a storm. The storm comes upon the wise man as severely as it does the foolish. In verse 25, Jesus describes the storm that comes to the wise man. Two verses later, He describes the storm that comes to the foolish man. The verses are identical.

There is pressure from above—*"the rains descended."* There is pressure from below—*"the floods came."* There is pressure from all sides—*"the winds blew."* Whether we're a saint or a sinner, we are going to experience the full range of what life brings. We're going to get pressed from above; pressed from below; pressed from all sides.

As Christians, we are not going to be exempt from the trials and the struggles, adversities, and pressures of life. Faith isn't tested in the sunshine; it is tested in the storm.

Each man built a house (a life). They experienced the same storm with the same severity, but that's where the similarity ends. Jesus makes it clear the difference wasn't in the design, architect, or the contractor. It wasn't in the interior décor or the exterior landscaping. The only difference was in the foundation.

One built his house and ignored the Word. When the storm came, his life collapsed. The other built his life by adhering to the Word. When the storm came, he stood strong.

This is where the entire Sermon on the Mount has been heading. Everything points to this one truth. There are many paths we can follow and many ideas we can consider. The difference between non-believers and followers of Jesus is not the problems we face; it's the way we respond to the problems.

What makes the difference between collapsing and standing is the foundation on which our life is built. The difference is in the standard by which we measure our life.

Two Loud Voices

It's no secret we live in a time in which the ideas of a solid foundation and an objective, absolute standard of measurement for life are being challenged by some very persuasive voices. One of the voices is that of *postmodern skepticism*. This view says there is no need for a foundation or a standard means of measuring because there is no such thing as absolute truth. What's true for you is whatever works for you at this moment. Your truth isn't necessarily my truth. Under this philosophy, everything is challenged. There is a huge skepticism about being able to find absolute truth.

Consequently, we find ourselves living in a time much like what is described in the Book of Judges, when every man did what was right in his own eyes (21:25). God's ways are deemed old-fashioned, quaint, and out of touch with modern reality. God's plan is either ignored outright or rejected as being too rigid. Flexibility is the key.

The other voice is closely akin to the first one. This is the *politically correct pluralism* of today. This voice argues you *do* need a foundation and a standard of measurement—but any foundation and standard will do. One means of measuring is as valid as the next. One foundation is as good as the next. All roads eventually lead to the same place.

This voice argues that everybody is inherently good. Sooner or later that goodness will surface, and when all is said and done, we'll live happily ever after. This is the voice of so-called "enlightenment and reason." The key is *tolerance*.

In response to the refrain that is being accepted by the popular influencers of our day, the message of the Bible rings out, *"There is a way which seems right to a man but its end is the way of death"* (Proverbs 14:12).

In this world you can choose from a plethora of available religions. There's Christianity, Orthodox Judaism, Islam, Buddhism, Hinduism, and a host of others. Even under the umbrella of Christianity there is a host of denominational stripes:

Baptist, Methodist, Presbyterian, Lutheran, Episcopalian,
Catholic, Nazarene, Mennonite, Christian Missionary Alliance,
Evangelical Free, African Methodist Episcopal (A.M.E.),
Assemblies of God, Church of God, Church of Christ, Church
of God in Christ . . . you get the picture.

In the final analysis, there are only two kinds of religion—
true and false. There are only two kinds of foundations—rock
and sand. Jesus said the way we would know if someone is
giving heed to the Word—building their life on the solid rock
of the Word—is by the fruit evidenced in their lives.

Root and Fruit

Any good farmer can tell you that the *root* produces the *fruit*.
If you have a tree bearing the wrong kind of fruit, there are a
lot of things you can do. You can prune it, but pruning won't
change the fruit. You can transplant it, but the fruit will remain
the same. You can cultivate it—same result. You can decorate
it—that may change the look but won't change the produce.
You can't change the fruit without changing the root.

Sometimes it's difficult to tell what kind of tree it is simply
by its appearance. There's one sure way to find out—wait
until it bears fruit. The root produces the fruit, and the fruit
reveals the root. If it bears peaches, it's a peach tree. If it bears
oranges, it's an orange tree. If you want to know something
about what kind of man or woman someone is, look at the
fruit they produce.

Many people hear the Word of God in church. It washes
over them week after week after week, but they aren't really
hearing it. They are not rooting their lives in it. They are not
using it as a standard by which to measure their lives. They
aren't building their lives on it.

I've checked the weather forecast, and if you're not in
the middle of one now, I can guarantee there's a storm in
your future. I don't know what the name of the storm will
be that strikes your life. It may be disease, financial reversal,

abandonment, abuse, fire, flood, or perhaps the death of a loved one. The question is, how are you going to respond when the storm comes? How are you going to survive? What plans are you making right now that will enable you to stand when everything around you is falling apart?

How are you going to handle it if your income is suddenly gone, and your savings are wiped out? Or if an accident leaves you broken? What about if your best friend becomes your worst enemy? How will you handle having all the support knocked out from under you? How will you cope when death suddenly takes a loved one?

We don't have an option about the storm, but we *do* have an option about how to respond when the storm hits. We can respond with fear or with faith. We can respond with despair or determination. We can respond with panic or with peace. We can collapse or we can conquer.

If we build our life on the shifting sand of what's popular in the marketplace and use that as the standard of measurement for our life, we'll collapse. The reason people build on the sand instead of the rock is because it's easier and cheaper.

Digging Deep

Luke's Gospel described the story like this: *"He is like a man building a house who <u>dug deep</u> and laid a foundation on the rock"* (6:45, emphasis added).

The reason most people don't get to a solid foundation is because they are not willing to do the heavy lifting. They're content to only "hear"—to have information about the Word—but they don't begin to put it into practice. Anybody can start putting up walls and a roof, but if we want it to stand when the storms of life come, we'll *dig deep*. We'll do more than just hear; we'll give heed to the Word.

The Word is more than just the printed words on the pages of a book we call the Bible. It isn't just the teachings of Jesus; it's His life. He is the incarnate Word—the living Word.

The foundation that is enduring, unchanging, unshakeable, secure, dependable isn't only the instructions of Jesus; it is the Lord Jesus himself.

When you live according to His will, His plan, His design, and His priorities, there is strength in the storm. There is peace that passes all comprehension. There is joy inexpressible and full of glory. There is hope that transcends this present temporal reality and looks into the realm of the eternal. There is faith that does not waver, and there is love that endures forever.

The only foundation worth staking your eternal life on is the standard and the foundation of the Lord Jesus. When every other foundation is shifting and sinking sand—unstable and passing away—the prophet proclaims in Malachi 3:6 that He is *"the Lord that does not change."* When every other standard is fluid and unreliable, Hebrews 13:8 declares He is *"the same yesterday, today, and forever."*

No matter how brutal the storm, there is hope. When you've anchored your faith and your trust in Jesus, no matter how fiercely the storm blows, you're going to survive. You're not going to collapse. You're not going under; you're going over. The valley you're in right now isn't the end of the story. The storm you're facing is not the final verdict. The negative report you've been given isn't the final, conclusive report.

As a child of God, you have a hope the world knows nothing about. You have a resource that never runs out. You have a help that never quits.

In Isaiah 40:28-31, the prophet wrote:

> Do you not know? Have you not heard? The Everlasting God, the Lord, the Creator of the ends of the earth does not become weary or tired. His understanding is inscrutable. He gives strength to the weary, and to him who lacks might He increases power. Though youths grow

weary and tired, and vigorous young men stumble badly, yet those who wait for the Lord will gain new strength; they will mount up with wings like eagles, they will run and not get tired, they will walk and not become weary.

In Isaiah 43:2-3a, God promises:

When you pass through the waters, I will be with you; and through the rivers, they will not overflow you. When you walk through the fire, you will not be scorched, nor will the flame burn you. For I am the Lord your God, the Holy One of Israel, your Savior.

You may be afflicted in every way right now, but according to 2 Corinthians 8:8, you're not going to be crushed. You may be perplexed, but you need not despair. You may be persecuted, but you're not forsaken. You may be struck down, but you won't be destroyed.

You may find yourself weeping, but according to Psalm 30:5, you'll have a shout of joy in the morning. You may find yourself falling, but according to Deuteronomy 33:27, underneath you'll feel God's *"everlasting arms."*

Every other foundation will crumble. Every other option will fail. But Jesus never fails. He will not let you fall!

Maybe we need to sing one more time, like we believe it:

On Christ, the solid rock I stand;
All other ground is sinking sand.
All other ground is sinking sand.

4

Selflessly Loving

It was a typical South Florida night in the summer of 1961. Hot. Muggy. Still. Dad and I had just walked across the yard from the parsonage next door to the little church he served as pastor to get ready for the Sunday-evening service. Before any of the congregation arrived, a man who looked to be in his early 40s timidly opened the door and peeked inside. Catching Dad's attention, he asked if he could speak with him.

This man was a migrant worker from the Bahamas, and was staying in a local camp just outside town to work in the sugarcane fields. He was a member of our denomination (Church of God), and was requesting permission to join us for worship that night. Today, that seems like a rather odd thing to do, but remember, this was 1961 in the South. We were a white congregation, and this was a black man.

Without hesitation, Dad answered, "Certainly, you're welcome to worship with us." The man entered, went to the back row, knelt for a few moments in prayer, and then sat in the pew reading his Bible until the service began.

About twenty minutes into the service, the choir was singing and the people were worshiping when a police officer entered the sanctuary and motioned for the man to come outside with him. From his vantage point on the platform, Dad observed what was happening and quickly exited through a side door. He arrived at the front of the church just as the policeman was preparing to place the now handcuffed man in the back of his squad car.

Seeing Dad hurrying to the car, the policeman rounded on him and said, "Preacher, what do you mean letting this (racial slur) in the church? Are you trying to start a riot!"

Pushing himself between the two men, Dad got in the face of the officer and demanded, "You let that man go right now! He's broken no laws. He asked permission to worship with us before ever entering the building, and I gladly granted it. Since he's been here, he's been more respectful and reverential of God's house than anybody else in the congregation. He's welcome to worship with us anytime he wants!"

Taking a step back, the officer paused for a moment and then said, "Well, I hope you know what you're doing; but if anything happens, it's all on you." Whereupon he removed the handcuffs, released the man, got in his car, and drove off.

Before escorting the man back into church, Dad asked him how he had gotten to church. Hearing that he had walked, Dad said, "When church is over, don't leave right away. I want to make sure there isn't somebody out there waiting to jump you to try and teach you a lesson. If you'll wait until I have a chance to lock up, I'll drive you back to the camp so you'll be protected."

That event took place over sixty years ago, but it is still as fresh in my mind as if it were yesterday. It was my first (unfortunately not my last) time to witness racism. Watching Dad's outrage over the injustice and his defense of one who was helpless made an indelible impression on my young mind; comparable, I suspect, to the impression made on the minds of those who first heard the story Jesus told in the Gospel of Luke, chapter 10.

A lawyer had approached Jesus with the question, *"Who is my neighbor?"* (v. 29). This lawyer wasn't an attorney in the sense we understand it today. He was an expert in interpreting religious laws and traditions—a master theologian. We soon discover he wasn't asking Jesus this question in order to gain information and clarity. Instead, verse 25 identifies his motive when it says he *"put [Jesus] to the test."* When Jesus answered, the lawyer asked a follow-up question, *"wishing to justify himself"* (v. 29).

In response to the question posed by the lawyer, Jesus told the parable of the Good Samaritan. If you're going to get the right answer to "Who is my neighbor?", it's critical to have the right point of view. The command of Jesus is, *Love your neighbor*. The question is, *Who is my neighbor?* The interpretive question is, *Whose viewpoint will we take?*

The Victim

Can you imagine acting like a lot of news reporters, going with microphone in hand and camera rolling to that man lying in a pool of blood and saying, "Pardon me, sir. We're doing a theological survey, and I wonder from your perspective down there in the ditch, who would you say is your neighbor?"

If the man could somehow manage to mumble a reply, his answer would be as wide as the world. Just about anybody coming down the road who was willing to stop and lend a hand would qualify.

You can relate. Here you are, driving down the road, and your car begins to make strange noises before it comes rolling to a stop. You don't have any tools with you, and even if you did, you don't have the skills to fix the problem. At that moment, just about anybody coming down the road who's willing to stop and lend a hand qualifies completely as a neighbor. However, when the other person's car has come to a stop and you're cruising along, it's easy to sit behind the wheel and define *neighbor* with all the preciseness of a shyster attorney.

The Priest and Levite

If the poor guy in the ditch was making a list of candidates for neighbor, I suspect a priest and a Levite would have been at the top. Tradition says before these guys left their house in the morning, they would have quoted the greatest commandment from the Bible: *"You shall love the Lord your God with all your heart, with all your soul, and with all your strength"* (Deuteronomy 6:5). It would seem the folks who were devoted to keeping and teaching the Law would have been filled with love for God, resulting in loving others.

But Jesus said the priest came down the road, saw the man, and passed by on the other side. It's hard to understand how that could happen. How could one human being see another human being in such desperate need and do absolutely nothing to help him?

Since the priest was religious, I'm sure his reasons were religious. In the Old Testament, the Law said if a priest touched a dead body, he would become ceremonially defiled. I imagine that priest thinking:

> I'd really like to help, but it would be just my luck to have this man haul off and die in my arms, and I'd have to go through all the cleansing rituals, and the sacrifice I'd have to offer is expensive. Not only that, but somebody might see me going through the ritual, and might start asking questions about what I'm being cleansed from. The whole thing could hurt my influence and damage my testimony.

I don't *know* that he thought that way. But I do know followers of Jesus sometimes get more concerned about what others will think about them than with reaching out and helping someone who is hurting.

The second man who came down the road was a Levite. If the priest was like a pastor, then the Levite was like an assistant pastor, or maybe the worship pastor. He took care of the scrolls, led the music, and sometimes did some of the teaching and other duties of ministry.

Jesus said the Levite saw the man and also passed by on the other side. Perhaps the Levite thought:

> I'm on my way to Jerusalem to give my lecture on neighborly love. This will make a great illustration for my teaching. I'll challenge the young people to start a

Jericho Road Missions Society. They'll get organized and have a ministry outreach to folks beaten up on the Jericho Road.

Followers of Jesus sometimes think like that. A unique kind of arithmetic is used to measure success in ministry. This arithmetic is always interested in reaching the masses, but somehow never gets down to individuals. This kind of arithmetic always talks about winning the world, but doesn't think much about winning a neighborhood. This kind of arithmetic makes it valiant to cross oceans, but never crosses streets.

Samaritan

We call this the parable of the Good Samaritan, but the man is never called "good." In that day, the words *good* and *Samaritan* didn't belong in the same sentence. It would be like calling someone an "honest thief" or a "faithful adulterer." If the priest and the Levite were at the top of the list of candidates for a neighbor, then the Samaritan was at the bottom . . . if he made the list at all.

An animosity had existed between the Jews and the Samaritans for hundreds of years. Jews referred to Samaritans as dogs. But when this Samaritan came down the road and saw the wounded man, he was filled with compassion. He dismounted from his donkey, got down in the ditch, and cleansed and bandaged the wounds of the injured man. He put the man on his donkey, took him to an inn, sat with him through the night, paid the room rent, and promised to pay for anything else that was needed in nursing this man back to health.

When Jesus finished the story, He asked, "Which of these three was neighbor to this man who was beaten up by thugs— the two who knew their theology, or the one who stopped to help?" The young lawyer, not even willing to say the word *Samaritan*, answered, *"The one who showed mercy on him"* (v. 37). Jesus said, *"Go and do likewise"* (v. 37).

Who is your neighbor? The answer is simple. **Your neighbor is anyone whose need you see and whose need you're in a position to meet**.

This has nothing to do with liking the person. Attraction isn't the issue. The issue is, are they in need and has God put you in a position to meet that need? **The extent of your love for Jesus can be measured by the amount of love you have for the person you love the least**.

If we'll open our eyes, we'll discover there are plenty of people lying in the ditch, but not nearly enough Samaritans to go around. We don't have to look very long or travel far to find a neighbor who needs us to extend God's love. So, why don't we get off our donkey and get into the ditch?

The Risk Factor

There was a risk attached to the good deed of this Samaritan. The journey from Jericho to Jerusalem was well known for its danger. It was steep and treacherous with many places for robbers to hide. A thief could lie on the side of the road, pretending to be injured, trying to lure someone to stop and check. Then he and his partners could jump the benevolent person, beat him up, rob him, and even kill him. This dangerous route became known as "the way of blood." The Samaritan was taking a huge risk when he stopped.

One of the reasons we are reluctant to help someone in the ditch is we're afraid it will cost us something. Truthfully, it *will* cost us something. It cost this Samaritan a lot—his time, his energy, lost wages, and maybe additional room and medical expenses.

There are other things he could have been risking. Was the Samaritan a businessman? The Bible says he was on a journey. Was it a business trip? Was he meeting a client in order to close a big account? Did he miss the appointment and lose the account?

I wonder if the man the ditch was overweight. Was the donkey old, on its last donkey legs? Those questions may seem strange, but they matter. Could the Samaritan afford a trip to the chiropractor if he pulled his back out trying to hoist the injured man onto his donkey? Could he afford a new donkey if something happened to this one? What if the donkey collapsed with the man on its back, and when the man got better, he sued the Samaritan for damages?

Sound ridiculous? No more ridiculous than some of the reasons we come up with for not reaching out to that person whose need God has put in front of us and given us the resources to meet.

Verse 33 says the Samaritan "had compassion." There's a difference between pity and compassion. Pity weeps and runs away; compassion comes to help and stay. There's a difference between charity and compassion. Charity is tax-deductible; compassion is time-consuming. **Compassion costs something**.

Race Factor
Jesus never identified the nationality or the ethnicity of the man in the ditch. We assume he was a Jew, but we are never told that for certain. In that culture, as in our own, clothes make the man. You can often tell something about a person's ethnicity, education, and earnings by the kind of garment he wears, but this man had been stripped naked.

We don't know if he was a Jew or a Gentile, wealthy or poor, conservative or liberal, good person or bad person. We don't know if he was part of a gang and did something that caused them to be upset with him, so they beat him and abandoned him. Or if he was an innocent traveler in the wrong place at the wrong time. What we see is just a naked, completely vulnerable, beaten person left for dead on the side of the road.

One thing we know is the victim was a human being. What if he was a Samaritan as well? What if he was black? Turn it around: What if he was white and the priest and the Levite were black? Had this story been told in our day, there are more variables we could consider. What if he was in our country illegally? What if he was gay, or trans? The possibilities keep piling up.

The tragedy is those who passed by saw this injured man as a nobody. When the Samaritan looked at the man lying in the ditch, however, I think he saw himself. There was an identification. He recognized if he had come to that place just a few minutes earlier, he could have been the one mugged, robbed, and left for dead.

This is how to deal with injustice in this world—to heal the hurts of the wounded, remove the tensions, tear down the walls, and build bridges across social, economic, and racial divides. It happens when we begin to see ourselves as the other person. It happens when we begin to understand, "There, but for the grace of God, go I."

Racism isn't solely a white problem, and it isn't solely a black problem. Racism is a human problem, and it's a spiritual problem. Racists don't want to hear someone of a different ethnicity is their neighbor. Conservatives don't want to hear illegal immigrants are their neighbors. Liberals don't want to hear unborn babies are their neighbors.

The lawyer came to Jesus seeking to *justify himself*. So maybe the question he should have asked—and the one nobody is willing to ask because it doesn't sound spiritual (but it's the one we want answered), is this: Who am I allowed to hate?

The Jericho Road was used by Jews to bypass Samaria. There were quicker routes, but most would rather risk their lives than chance coming into contact with the hated Samaritans. It makes me wonder what the priest and Levite were doing on that road in the first place. In reality, the Jericho Road was a hiding place for hate.

The lawyer was hoping Jesus would give him an out for his hate. (If Jesus would set the limits of "my neighbor" to those who look, dress, and behave like me, then I will have justification or permission to hate those who don't look, talk, dress, or act like me.) With this story, Jesus slams the door on every escape route. His response to the question makes it clear that neither geography, ethnicity, culture, nor anything else is an adequate reason to hate. Nobody gets a permission-to-hate card!

Dialogue. Vote. Petition. Even protest. Do everything you can to insure justice and equality. Challenge the status quo. Don't allow tradition to cloud your sight from seeing when something is wrong. Stand for truth. Refuse to participate in anything that dehumanizes or deprives another of dignity and value, but in the midst of it all, hate is not an option. You can't stop violence with violence. You can't solve hate with hate.

There are no loopholes to allow you to hate any group. Not the drug dealers or the drug addicts; not the gays or the adulterers; not the people in another denomination; not those who did you wrong; not the liars or the heart-breakers; not the people in law enforcement; not the protesters. No loopholes!

> If anyone boasts, "I love God," and goes right on hating his brother or sister, thinking nothing of it, he is a liar. If he won't love the person he can see, how can he love the God he can't see? The command from God is blunt: Loving God includes loving people. You've got to love both (1 John 4:20-21 MSG).

Relationship Factor

All three characters in the story saw a stranger who had been mugged and left in the ditch to die, but in a sense, they didn't really see the same thing. Buried within this story lies a deeper truth: What you **are** determines what you **see**.

Christian love doesn't reside in the person being loved; rather, it resides in the person doing the loving. The way God continues to love us, even when we stray from His will and violate His commands, is because He is a loving God. He doesn't love us because we're such lovable people; He loves us because He's such a loving God.

Sometimes our neighbors aren't too lovable. So, how can we love still them? The answer is we are able to continue to love both in word and in deed because love doesn't reside in the object of love. Love resides in the person doing the loving.

I know that looks good on paper, but let's be real—sometimes that's hard! There is a bias within the human heart. Jeremiah 17:9 says, *"The heart is deceitful above all things, and desperately wicked."* No matter how hard we aim at the target of doing and thinking and acting right, we always seem to miss it. God looks deep inside our heart, which thinks thoughts God would rather we not think. Our heart decides to do things God would not have us do. By itself, the human heart isn't capable of loving God or a neighbor. Because our heart is so diseased, the only hope for things to be different is for us to have a heart transplant. This is the promise of Ezekiel 11:19-20:

> And I shall give them one heart, and shall put a new spirit within them. And I shall take the heart of stone out of their flesh and give them a heart of flesh, that they may walk in My statutes, and keep My ordinances, and do them. Then they will be My people, and I shall be their God.

To have a transplant, there must be a donor. A number of years ago, a call went out in our community for a donor of bone marrow that would match a person who was in dire need. I went to the blood center, had my blood typed, and put my name on the registry of possible donors. I wasn't a match for that person, but the possibility exists that someday I might be a match for someone needing the particular characteristics of my blood and marrow.

I have a friend who found out about a mutual friend who needed a kidney transplant. He went through the tests and found his kidney would be compatible, and he gladly donated one of his so the friend could survive.

Bone marrow replenishes, so if I donate, I haven't lost anything. My friend lives an active, normal life with a single kidney. But how many people do you know who would say, "You need a heart? Take mine!" I only know one person like that.

When God looked down at the human race and saw only a transplant would do, Jesus, the only begotten Son of the Father said, "Take My heart." On an operating table in the shape of a cross, the Great Physician lifted out the heart and nature of Jesus and offered it to the world. He offered His heart because He knew our hearts would never love God and would certainly never love our neighbor. When we, as the Bible says, *become partakers of the divine nature* through a heart transplant (2 Peter 1:4)—when we receive the heart of Jesus, then all the valves are open.

Only when we have had a heart transplant can we begin to live out the command to love our neighbor. Only with a new heart can we be selfless, loving followers of Jesus.

> As a young child, I learned this nursery rhyme:
> Pussycat, pussycat, where have you been?
> I've been to London to see the Queen;
> Pussycat, pussycat, what saw you there?
> I saw a wee mousy under her chair.

This cat was surrounded by the splendor of the palace—beautiful tapestries, smartly uniformed guards, and awe-inspiring architecture. He was in the presence of nobility and royalty, but when he gave his report about his experience, there was no mention of beauty and wealth and royalty. All he could talk about was seeing a mouse under the throne.

Do you know why that's all he could talk about? Because he was a cat. He saw with cat eyes. He had the motivation of a cat and the priorities of a cat. Before he could really see anything else around him, he would need a different heart.

The same is true for us. Before we can truly see and respond to the needs and hurts of those around us, we must have a different heart. We must have a heart that beats in sync with the heart of the heavenly Father. We need a heart transplant. Only then will we be able to respond in obedience to the command of our Lord to selflessly love our neighbor, demonstrating what it means to be a follower of Jesus.

5

Daily Worshiping

It's not possible to talk about the essentials necessary to be a true follower of Jesus without talking about worship. We use the word *worship* a lot in the church, but too many don't understand the scope of what's involved. We talk about the time we spend together as a "worship service." We employ people on staff with the title of "worship pastor." When we talk about worship, many people immediately think of the music portion of the time spent in church on Sunday morning or a concert featuring their favorite Christian artist. However, the Bible does not talk about worship as an event, but instead as a lifestyle.

When the Apostle Paul wrote his letter to the church at Rome, he spent the first 11 chapters laying out the doctrine of the Gospel. He explained how the whole world was guilty before God and how humanity could be reconciled to God only through Jesus. He talked about genuine righteousness, explaining it first as the righteousness God himself possesses and manifests in all His actions, and then as the righteousness He gives to human beings by grace through faith.

God *imputes* righteousness, which creates a right standing before Him, known as *justification*. Then God *imparts* righteousness in practice, known as *regeneration*. Further, God imparts a progressively transformed lifestyle through the indwelling of the Holy Spirit, known as *sanctification*.

At the end of this doctrinal proclamation, overwhelmed by the magnitude of the Lord's marvelous work and the depth of His glory, the apostle breaks into an outburst of adoration in 11:33-36. He writes a doxology of praise to celebrate the majesty of God's redemptive work.

In chapter 12, he proceeds to write about how theology is to inform practice. He says in light of all God has done for us, here's how we ought to respond. The relationship we have with God is not compartmentalized into sacred and secular. At the same time, worship isn't accidental or uniformed. It isn't some ritual to be performed or some tradition to be mindlessly observed.

When Paul talks about the kind of worship that is the hallmark of Jesus' followers, he reaches back into ancient times when worship was instituted in the Old Testament. He says the kind of worship that has transformational ability is sacrificial worship. Unlike the Old Testament practice, however, this sacrificial worship isn't an event on certain holy days; it's a lifestyle.

Reason for Sacrificial Worship—The Mercies of God
Paul appeals to *"the mercies of God"* (12:1), referring to God's multitude of mercies. Most people seem to think they have to meet certain criteria or expectations to get God's mercy. That isn't the way it works. God gives a multitude of mercies apart from anything you do. With God, mercy isn't a one-and-done proposition. God isn't just merciful once, but again . . . again . . . and again. He has consistently and constantly demonstrated His mercy toward you, even when you weren't aware of it.

Put on your imagination cap, pretending you are in a theater with a giant IMAX screen. You have a jumbo tub of popcorn in your lap and a large soft drink in the cup holder beside you. Playing on the screen, in high definition, is scene after scene of times God's mercy has been extended to you. Think about the images that would parade across that screen.

Pastor Mark Batterson says the prerequisite to worship is mercy:

> And the prerequisite to mercy is doing something
> wrong. So, if you've done something wrong you qualify
> for mercy. And if you qualify for mercy you qualify for

worship. . . . Don't let what's wrong with you keep you
from worshiping what's right with God.

Even before you were part of the household of faith, the
mercy of God was reaching to you. His mercy called to you
and marked you for salvation. When you tried to run from
Him, His mercy kept coming after you. At times when you
should have gotten into major trouble, His mercy spared you.
Certain experiences that you chalked up to good fortune, or a
twist of fate, or the results of your own ingenuity were actually
the mercies of God.

God's mercy sent Jesus to this earth to be your Savior. His
mercy brought you to a place where you could hear the Gospel.
His mercy gave you the faith to believe and surrender your
life to Jesus.

Since you've been a follower of Jesus, God's mercy has kept,
sustained, and protected you. Every time you've stumbled
and failed, His mercy has picked you up. Every time you've
wandered off the path and gone the wrong direction, His
mercy has turned you around and put you on the upward way.

Because of His mercy, you have a roof over your head,
clothes on your body, shoes on your feet, and food on your
table. You have warm blood flowing in your veins. You woke
up this morning in your right mind. You have joy in your soul
and peace in your heart. You have help for today and hope
for tomorrow all because of the mercy of God.

Long after you've eaten the last kernel of popcorn and
taken the last sip of soda, the mercies of God in your life will
still be scrolling across the screen. *"The mercy of the Lord is from
everlasting to everlasting on those who fear Him, and His righteousness
to children's children"* (Psalm 103:17). The Apostle Paul would
say in light of the manifold mercies of God, the only logical,
reasonable response is a lifestyle of sacrificial worship. Maybe
you should stop reading for a moment and give thanks for His
mercies that have been extended to your life.

Requirement of Sacrificial Worship—Living Sacrifice

The phrase *"living sacrifice"* (Romans 12:2) is an *oxymoron*—a combination of two seemingly contradictory or incongruous words.

Sacrifices in the Old Testament were slaughtered animals, but Paul transformed the idea of *sacrifice* into something alive and active. The worship we are to offer God retains the essential elements of Old Testament sacrifice, but it has changed from dead ritual to living lifestyle. When we look at the characteristics of Old Testament sacrifices, we begin to get a picture of what it means to offer ourselves as a *living sacrifice*.

Costly

In the Old Testament sacrificial system, the sacrifice was always the *finest* you had to give. No blind sheep or lame cattle were acceptable. In addition, the sacrifice was always brought in worship *first*. Worshipers brought the *firstborn* of their flock or herd. Before eating any of the crop, they brought the first-fruits of the harvest in worship as a thanksgiving and a reminder that God was first in their life.

The Message Bible paraphrases Romans 12:1: *"Take your everyday, ordinary life—your sleeping, eating, going-to-work, and walking-around life—and place it before God as an offering."*

There is no such thing as a partial sacrifice or commitment. It's impossible to be "sort of" committed.

Once, a pig and a chicken were walking down the road together. As they traveled, they came upon a sign advertising a breakfast to benefit the poor. The chicken said to the pig, "We should donate to that worthy cause. How about if I give an egg and you provide the ham?"

"Not so fast," replied the pig. "For you to give an egg would just be a contribution, but for me to give the ham would require a total commitment."

This is the problem with too many of us who claim to be followers of Jesus. Many are willing to make a contribution to the cause, but few are willing to give their total commitment. It's hard to get people to even be committed to something as simple as regular church attendance. While commitment to God and the church is deeper than attendance on Sunday, that's a good place to begin.

The cost of a *living sacrifice* isn't just the time we spend in church on Sunday. It's in the choices we make in the places we hang out and the people with whom we associate. It's in the decisions we make and the influences we allow to speak into our lives. It's in the way we spend our time, our money, and our energy. It's in living by one overriding question: *Lord, what will You have me to do?*

Consecrated

Paul says we should present our bodies a living and *holy* sacrifice. Most people hear the word *holy* and immediately think *sinless*. That isn't what it means. Holy simply means "set apart"—*consecrated* for a specific purpose.

It's true we are **in** the world, but we are not **of** the world. We're set apart from the world. We have different priorities, different allegiances, different motivations. As followers of Jesus, we are set apart for righteous purposes, which means we can't give ourselves to anything else. We can't give ourselves to things of the Spirit on Sunday and then to things of the flesh the rest of the week.

Too many are trying to make a false distinction between the material part and the spiritual part. They're happy to give God their hearts . . . as long as their eyes, hands, feet, and tongues are allowed to do what they please; but that is not a "living sacrifice" lifestyle of worship.

When we're holy, consecrated, and set apart, we don't belong to ourselves any longer; instead, we belong to the Lord. We aren't like the world around us; we have a different way of living.

- When the world is greedy, we're generous.

- When the world is dishonest, we're people of integrity.
- When the world is filled with hatred, we express love.
- While the world lives to please itself, we live to please God.
- When the world is immoral, we're committed to purity.
- When the world is negative, we're positive.
- When the world is fearful, we're confident.
- When the world is violent, we're peaceful.
- When the world is chaotic, we're calm.
- When the world is pessimistic, we're hopeful.
- When the world is aimlessly drifting, we're anchored.

True worship is more than giving up a couple of hours on Sunday to give lip service to a creed. True worship is offering our body as a living sacrifice in consecration. The work of our hands, the thoughts of our mind, the intentions of our heart—all of it is set apart for the Lord.

Constrained

The problem with a "living" sacrifice is that it has a tendency to crawl off the altar when the fire gets hot. On the corners of the Old Testament sacrificial altar were horns or hooks to which the offering would be tied in order to keep it from sliding off. Likewise, when we are a living sacrifice, we are bound to the sacrificial altar by two hooks—*devotion* and *discipline*. Lives are unrestrained when they are missing those two ingredients.

We don't make commitments and we don't get involved because we don't want to be bound down. We want the message to inspire and encourage, but when it creates an inconvenience or a challenge to our lifestyle, we casually toss it in the "reject" bin because we don't want to be bound to the requirements of righteousness. We try to judge the truth of the Word by our own experiences rather than judging our experiences by the Word. We're driven by feelings and emotion rather than by spirit and truth.

Consumed

When this costly, consecrated sacrifice is constrained on the altar, it is consumed. This is the essence of worship. Worship is putting yourself on the altar and letting God consume you. Being a living sacrifice unto God means we aren't serving ourselves; we're serving Him. We call the time assembled with other believers a "worship service," but when we are a living sacrifice, it gets changed and becomes "service worship."

I'm convinced God is less concerned about how our service time goes on Sunday morning and more concerned with how our service of worship goes outside the walls of the sanctuary. This is the *"spiritual service of worship."* It's what happens Monday through Saturday as we engage the service of worship. We pick up the towel and the basin, look for needs, and give without anyone knowing what we're doing. God isn't looking for us to lie on the altar as a dead sacrifice, but rather to live out our life selflessly for Him as a living sacrifice through the service of worship.

Results of Sacrificial Worship—Transformation and Revelation

"Don't let the world around you squeeze you into its own mold," is how J. B. Phillips paraphrased Romans 12:2. *The Message* paraphrases it, *"Don't become so well-adjusted to your culture that you fit into it without even thinking."*

When we offer ourselves as a living sacrifice, there's going to be a change in us. Instead of being *conformed* to the world, we're going to be *transformed*. It's the word from which we get *metamorphosis*. *Meta*, meaning "change"; *morphis*, meaning "form." It's a change of form.

In biology, we learn *metamorphosis* is the process that occurs when a caterpillar crawls into a cocoon and transforms into a beautiful butterfly. The inner nature of that caterpillar is that of a butterfly, and through the process of *metamorphosis* the inner nature is revealed.

53

The same word was used of Jesus when He was *transfigured* on the mount (Mark 9:1-3). Had you seen Jesus walking down the street before or after that event, you wouldn't have considered His appearance unusual. You probably would have walked right past Him. Judas had to point Him out so soldiers could arrest Him in Gethsemane (Matthew 26:28-29). The prophet Isaiah said, *"There was nothing beautiful or majestic about his appearance, nothing to attract us to him"* (Isaiah 53:2 NLT).

When people paint pictures of Jesus, they're using their imagination and taking artistic license. He didn't have light glowing from Him, neither did He have a halo around His head. He was an ordinary-looking person. If you saw Him, you wouldn't have picked Him out of the crowd. But, on the Mount of Transfiguration, the Bible says He began to glow like the sun and His garments became white as snow. There was a radiance about Him. The inner nature of Jesus was Deity, and on that mount, He was transfigured, and His inner nature came to the surface.

In the same way, the inner nature of a disciple is Jesus. This present age is trying to cancel the Jesus in you—or at least stuff Him in and silence Him. It doesn't want Jesus to come out. It's trying to <u>con</u>form you so you won't be <u>trans</u>formed—so your inner nature won't come to the surface. When your lifestyle is that of a living sacrifice, then you are transformed, and the inner nature of Jesus comes to the surface and people see Jesus in you.

With transformation comes *revelation*. It's a renewing of our mind that helps us *"prove what is that good and acceptable and perfect will of God"* (v. 2). Renewing the mind involves changing the way we think.

Changing the output of your thoughts is accomplished by changing the input. Studies have shown if you're an average American, you'll spend 1,000 hours this year watching television. Over a 65-year period, that means you would have spent 15 years watching television! By contrast, if you go to church every Sunday of your life for 65 years, you'll have spent eight months receiving spiritual training. Eight months compared to 15 years . . . and we wonder why we have such a hard time living with a spiritual mindset!

The grammar of this instruction about renewing the mind in the original language indicates it is not a one-time event, but an ongoing practice. It's something we have to do every day.

Here's what I know: From the moment we're born . . . through the years spent growing up . . . during all the time spent in school . . . through all the time spent in the workforce—everywhere we turn, the world is singing its siren song of indoctrination. It's pushing, pulling, squeezing, molding us into people who embrace the values and priorities of a fallen world alienated from God. But when we surrender our life to Jesus, turning from the ways of this world to embrace the Jesus way, according to 2 Corinthians 5:17, *"old things have passed away . . . all things have become new."*

As this living-sacrifice worship becomes a lifestyle and we actively renew our mind each day through inputting the truth of God's Word, our life stops *conforming* to the natural and becomes *transformed* into the supernatural.

- We stop living by feelings and start living by the truth of God's Word.
- We stop living by habit and start living by hope.
- We stop living by external pressure and start living by the Spirit.
- We stop living by fear and start living by faith.

That's when our life becomes acceptable to God. It has meaning and purpose, wholeness and completeness. Our life puts the glory of God's mercy in Jesus Christ on display for the world to see.

A number of years ago I read about the *Koh-i-Noor* diamond, which is part of the crown jewels of England. When this diamond was found, it was 186 carats. The value of this diamond was worth one-half the daily expenses of the whole world! This diamond was passed around until finally it ended up in India, under the aegis of a 10-year-old Punjab prince. The prince, in turn, was forced to place this diamond in the hands of England's Queen Victoria as part of a treaty.

A legend says after this Punjab prince grew to be a man, he went to where the jewels were kept and asked to see the *Koh-i-Noor* diamond. They brought it out for him. He then said, "Would you place it in my hand?" The prince then turned to the queen and said, "When I was a lad, I placed this diamond in your hands. I didn't know then what it was worth. Now, as a man, fully realizing its value, I want to again place it into your hands, my queen."

That's what Paul's message about a living sacrifice is all about. When I gave my heart to Jesus, I didn't fully understand what it meant. However, as I have grown in the grace and knowledge of Jesus—realizing all He has done for me and thinking of the mercies of God—I want to say what the prince said. Realizing so much more about Jesus and about me, I want to say, "Lord. I give you my life afresh and anew."

As you present yourself as a living sacrifice unto the Lord, you are transformed into someone whose life has meaning and purpose. Through being a living sacrifice you can tangibly demonstrate *"what is the good, acceptable, and perfect will of God"* (Romans 12:2). You will be marked as a true and faithful follower of Jesus, able to offer the help a hurting world desperately needs.

6

Humbly Serving

Every July 4th, this nation hits the pause button on its normal activities and routines to observe Independence Day. On this day we mark the formal signing of the Declaration of Independence—the formal proclamation of our liberties as United States citizens, and a symbol of freedom.

Since that historic day in 1776, the concept of freedom has been expanded to include not just freedom from oppression and tyranny from foreign powers, but the preservation of personal freedom as well. The concept of personal freedom has been relentlessly pursued in this country until it has, in many ways, become our national religion.

Personal freedom is inherently selfish. It focuses on "I" instead of "you" or "we." It demands rights. Personal freedom pushes to the head of the line. It's always on the lookout for any slight, either real or imagined. Personal freedom ignores rules it considers inconvenient or unnecessary because, after all, who are you to tell me what I can and cannot do? Personal freedom is easily offended. It is intolerant of opposing viewpoints.

United Sate citizens are committed to the ideal of personal freedom and are fiercely independent. That's the American way, but it isn't the Jesus way.

In Paul's letter to the church at Philippi, he said followers of Jesus are supposed to have the same attitude—the same *"mind"*—as Jesus (2:5). In verses 6 and 7, he says this attitude is the opposite of fierce independence and personal freedom. Instead, the attitude of the true follower of Jesus is to be that of a servant.

In verses 6-8, Paul used the words *"form," "likeness,"* and *"appearance"* in describing Jesus' life on earth. In our English language those words are almost interchangeable; however, the original language of the New Testament used two different words with distinct meanings.

The first word, *morphe*, describes an essential form that never alters. The second word *schema*, refers to an outward form or shape that changes from time to time and from circumstance to circumstance.

The *morphe* of myself and other people is humanity, which never changes; but my *schema* has changed considerably as I've grown and matured over the 67-plus years I've been alive. I began as an infant, grew to an adolescent, developed into a middle-aged man, and now have matured into a seasoned (translated "old") man. I have always had the same *morphe* (humanity), but my outward *schema* changes all the time.

In verse 6, the word *morphe* is used in declaring Jesus existed *"in the* form *of God."* That means His unchangeable being is Deity. No matter where He is or what He is doing, Jesus is always, unchangeably, and unalterably divine.

Even though His *morphe* never changes, His *schema* might alter. Verse 7 says Jesus took on *"the form* [the likeness, the *schema*] *of a bondservant."* He was *"found in appearance [schema] as a man"* (v. 8). Whether in Heaven or on earth, whether adored by angels or persecuted by men, and whether received reverently or rejected violently, Jesus always retains His divinity. His outward appearance (*schema*) may change, but His nature and essential character (*morphe*) never does. These two words help to inform our understanding of the magnitude of the sacrifice Jesus made by becoming a servant.

Verse 8 says Jesus *"humbled Himself."* Jesus started at the absolutely highest position that can be held—He is God. Being *"in the form (morphe) of God"* (v. 6) means a spiritual being who is Himself God. Jesus is not an assistant or a junior partner to God. Jesus has never been vice-president of Heaven. Instead, Jesus is equal with the Almighty Father and the Holy Spirit in every way.

Colossians 1:16-18 talks about this in describing Jesus:

> For by Him all things were created, both in the heavens and on earth, visible and invisible, whether thrones or dominions or rulers or authorities —all things have been created by Him and for Him.
>
> And He is before all things, and in Him all things hold together.
>
> He is also head of the body, the church; and He is the beginning, the first-born from the dead; so that He Himself might come to have first place in everything.

From the highest position possible, Jesus *emptied Himself* (v. 7). Jesus relaxed His grip on all the privileges afforded Him in order to become a man.

We cannot fully describe or even imagine what a violent and profane transition it was for the God of the universe to divest Himself of glory, relax His grip on privilege, empty Himself of all that would hinder the transition, and take on the appearance and be made in the likeness of a man. When this transcendent Creator took on the appearance and likeness of the creature, He did not appear on the landscape of this planet as an emperor or king. He did not come as a statesman or an investment banker. He was not part of the aristocracy. He did not have any of the trappings of privilege, power, or prestige; He showed up on this planet as a helpless baby, born in a stable to a blue-collar Jewish family.

Jesus—the omniscient, omnipresent, omnipotent, second person of the Trinity—was fully God, enjoying all the divine prerogatives from eternity. But as a man, He felt the binding confines and restrictions of flesh. He had to open doors, ride animals, eat meals, and sleep. He was dependent upon and submitted to earthly parents. The Creator of the universe rubbed shoulders with His creatures—the people He created. But His humbling process was not complete.

Verse 8 says He went even further by humbling Himself and becoming *"obedient to the point of death."* Jesus—the One who breathed life into all that lives. Jesus—the One who initiated all life in the universe and sustains it every second of every day. This Jesus stood face-to-face with the power of death and gave up without even a fight.

But even that was not enough, for verse 8 adds it was not just any kind of death, but *"the death of the cross."* This mode of execution didn't simply kill men, but first humiliated them and then tortured them slowly so every sensation of dying would be intensified and experienced in the fullest measure. While all that was going on, common men and women—the very ones He had created—could walk by and laugh, spit, throw sticks and rocks at Him, and hurl ugly accusations that made the hellishness complete.

Every bit of this downward slide from the glories of Heaven to the humbling, torturous death on a cross was not something done **to** Him. Rather, it came as a direct action from Jesus himself. There is no hint He was helpless and powerless, or a victim of circumstances beyond His control. Instead, each step from Heaven to the cross was intentionally taken.

In John 10:17-18, Jesus said:

> For this reason the Father loves Me, because I lay down My life so that I may take it again. No one has taken it away from Me, but I lay it down on My own initiative. I have authority to lay it down, and I have authority to take it up again.

If anyone had a right to be fiercely independent and insist on personal freedom, it was Jesus. Yet He took one intentional step after another—no matter how distasteful, painful, or abhorrent—that brought Him closer and closer to His cross. He did not take those steps of humiliation for Himself but for you and for me. His focus was on us.

In Philippian 2:3-4, Paul wrote: *"Do nothing from selfishness or empty conceit, but with humility consider one another as more important than yourselves; do not merely look out for your own personal interests, but also for the interests of others."*

This isn't just a theological treatise or a doctrinal proposition. This is a practical message with practical implications for where we live today. This message of servanthood speaks to family members in the home. It speaks to employers and employees on the job. It speaks to the church in the midst of an unbelieving world. It speaks to every arena of life on every level of living.

We are to have the attitude toward life that Jesus had. We are to think of ourselves the way Jesus thought of Himself. The problem is we're too busy thinking of ourselves. We're "clutchers." We clutch power when we're able to obtain it. We clutch possessions and resources, positions and titles, acclaim and affirmation. We look for recognition. We are consumed with making sure no one takes advantage of us. We demand our rights. We protest injustices and offenses.

The example of Jesus says, "Give up! Don't insist on your own way. Honor one another. Prefer one another. Humble yourself, even when it means part of you dies in the process."

True leaders aren't necessarily those with the title of "leader." The best servants are the genuine leaders.

I hear a lot of talk in the marketplace and even in the church about a leadership crisis. The truth is we don't have a leadership crisis, but a servanthood crisis. Our problem is articulated in the words of an old country gospel song: "Nobody wants to play rhythm guitar behind Jesus."

Too many of us want to lead the parade . . . get the corner office . . . receive the title . . . hear the applause . . . grasp for power . . . insist on perks . . . boast in prestige. There aren't nearly enough people willing to work behind the scenes or wash dirty feet.

Marriages get in trouble when both the husband and the wife are looking for what they're going to get out of the relationship and not willing to put their spouse first. People get dissatisfied with the church when they're coming to for what they're going to get out of it. Feed me. Care for me. Notice me. Affirm me. Visit me. Call me. Make me feel good.

People are unfulfilled on their jobs. Far too many think work is what they do so they can get to the weekend. They've forgotten they're not just working for a paycheck or for advancement in a career, but they're working as unto the Lord.

Followers of Jesus ought to be the best workers in the company. We may work for an earthly company, but behind the earthly master stands the heavenly Master. Behind your boss stands *the* Boss. Behind the chairman of the board stands the Chairman of the universe. If you're just working for a career or a paycheck or an earthly boss, you're wasting your life.

When we do a good job, we're serving Jesus as much as a missionary on the other side of the globe. Perhaps the best place for our faith to shine is in the marketplace where we're rubbing shoulders every day with people who don't know Jesus. That's why Jesus said, "*You are the salt of the earth. . . . You are the light of the earth*" (Matthew 5:13-14).

It's a lot easier to talk about being a servant than it is to put it into practice. Thankfully, Jesus not only told us *what* to do; He also showed us *how* to do it. In John 13, on the night Jesus was preparing to face His greatest struggle, the plan for His betrayal was in motion and the cross was before Him. When everyone around Him was calling Him Master and Lord, Jesus didn't reach for a title; He reached for a towel:

> Jesus, knowing that the Father had given all things into
> His hands, and that He had come forth from God and
> was going back to God, rose from supper and laid aside
> His garments, took a towel and girded Himself (vv. 3-4).

Who You Are—Identity

One of the greatest challenges we face as followers of Jesus is the issue of identity. Jesus knew! He didn't have to prove anything. He knew the Father had given all things into His hands. He knew He had come from God. He knew who He was. This is foundational to being able to fulfill the command to serve with humility. .

Do you know who you are? I don't mean the name that was assigned to you and placed on your birth certificate. I don't mean what's on your driver's license, your passport, or your paycheck. Do you know who you are in Jesus?

According to 2 Corinthians 5:17, if you have repented of your sin . . . if you have surrendered your life to Jesus . . . if you are *in Christ* . . . you are a *"new creation; old things have passed away; behold, all things have become new."*

According to Galatians 3:26, if you have put your faith in Jesus, you're not just a child of your biological parents; you're also a child of God. Verse 27 says you *"have clothed yourselves with Christ."* According to verse 28, there's a change in your ethnic identity—in Christ, *"there is neither Jew nor Greek."* There's been a change in your social identity—*"there is neither slave nor free."* In Christ, men and women are equals—*"there is neither male nor female."*

The primary identifier of our life isn't skin color or gender. It isn't social standing or the amount of assets we possess. The primary identifier is we are followers of Jesus.

Why You Are Here—Purpose

Jesus understood His purpose was to serve. He told His followers, *"For even the Son of Man did not come to be served, but to serve, and to give His life a ransom for many"* (Mark 10:45).

When we are submitted to Jesus His purpose becomes our purpose. His mission becomes our mission. The idea isn't to look down on our neighbors to try to save them; rather, it's to look up to them to serve them. The problem is sin has blown all the circuit-breakers. None of us are servants by nature. It requires the transforming power of the Holy Spirit. It requires an intentional surrender of our will to His will. The people who make God's best-dressed list are the towel-wearers and the basin-bearers.

When we intentionally serve, we have the ability to change the atmosphere wherever we are. I wonder what would happen if we responded to anger with a plate of homemade cookies? Or if we responded to someone spreading slander by washing their car? What if we responded to the malicious gossip by raking their leaves and mowing their grass? Or if we responded to ridicule and persecution by giving away tickets to the game? What would happen if we stopped seeing ourselves as put on this earth to get everybody straightened out and started seeing ourselves as being placed on this planet for the purpose of serving?

Where You're Going—Destiny
Before reaching for the towel, John 13:3 says Jesus knew He was *"going back to God"* (NASB). Jesus was able to leave the splendor of Heaven and face the most horrible death imaginable because He knew where He was going.

In the same way, whatever darkness comes our way, we are able to serve when we are certain of our destiny. The only way to be certain our eternal dwelling place will be in the celestial city of God is to surrender our life to Jesus.

With our life secure in Jesus, we can joyfully serve others, recognizing our trials and hardships and disappointments are only temporary. This world is not our final destination. We truly are pilgrims and strangers. Our destiny is with Jesus; we are ultimately going back to God. Until then, as followers of Jesus, we must humbly serve others.

7

Family Centered

It's no revelation for me to say we live in difficult times. Everywhere we go, people are on edge. Emotions are stretched to the breaking point. Pressures are mounting. Fear is prevalent. Weariness has settled in. Problems seem insurmountable. The one place that is supposed to be best suited to deal with the stress and pressure of this age is facing the greatest challenge. I'm talking about the family. Instead of the family being a safe and secure shelter from the storms of life, it has come under fire, and the fabric of society is being torn apart.

In his mini-book *The Jesus Manifesto*, Michael Brown wrote:

> The last generation's counterculture of rebellion has become this generation's establishment of revulsion, and what was unthinkable thirty years ago—daytime talks shows celebrating adultery and incest; homosexual love scenes on major network TV . . . massacres in our schools and houses of worship—is a matter of course today.

In an article in *The Christian Post,* Brown writes about a cultural shift and the rise of what he calls "mobocracy"—where the most radical elements of society forcefully impose their will on everyone else.

Families today are experiencing the pressure of the *relative morals of the times,* in which we are told there are no objective standards of absolutes.

Families are experiencing *social pressures*—a great deal of stress trying to measure up to the definition of *success* being hailed by our world.

Families are experiencing the pressure of *behavioral inconsistencies,* where actions are not in keeping with what is being said and taught.

Quite possibly the greatest pressure is *spiritual indifference*—God's standard is being ignored and replaced by a do-it-yourself brand of faith where anything you want to believe is acceptable. Instead of sincerely praying to Almighty God, we now send "positive thoughts" and "good vibes."

These pressures have brought us to the place where we have a breakdown of moral purity that has resulted in unwanted pregnancies and aborted children. We have throwaway relationships, divorce on demand, absentee fathers, and abused and abandoned children. The family unit has been redefined until it bears no resemblance to the original design of the heavenly Father of one man married to one woman until parted by death.

In the midst of this chaos, we need principles that will strengthen and encourage true followers of Jesus. These principles will set us apart from unbelievers and create families that will demonstrate to an unregenerate world what a real family can and should be.

We Need Leadership

Success or failure in every arena of life rises and falls on leadership. One of the biggest reasons troubles exist in families today is because, in many cases, parents have abdicated their leadership roles. Parents have looked to television and gaming stations to be their children's babysitters, the schools to be their children's teachers, and the church to be their children's spiritual guide. Consequently, we have an entire generation mired in confusion about even such basic things as defining *male* and *female.* People have lost the ability to differentiate between moral and immoral, good and evil.

If there is going to be real leadership in the family, then there are some critical ingredients that must be in place.

Time

There is no substitute for fathers and mothers spending time with their children, and it won't do to talk about *quality* instead of *quantity*. The amount of time is important! There has to be an intentionality about the time we spend and the input we give. Look for teachable moments: *"when you sit in your house, when you walk by the way, when you lie down, and when you rise up"* (Deuteronomy 6:7).

This isn't just taking time to tell the children what I want them to know. It also means investing the time to get to know them—their likes and dislikes, their desires, their frustrations and fears—what makes them tick.

Availability

No matter how busy we are, we dare not be too busy for our children. It means being available when they have something troubling them, or when they have a success they can't wait to share.

Modeling

Being a pastor gives me a unique place from which to observe family dynamics. With some families, I wonder who the parent is. When the family stays out of church because Junior didn't want to go today, who's the parent? When the credit card is overextended because the little princess wanted something they couldn't afford, but she insisted she needed it to be happy, who's the parent? When life revolves around every whim and desire of the child, who's the parent?

Maybe you grew up in a home with parents who were not great role models, but that doesn't mean you have to follow the same path. You can draw a line in the sand today and determine that from this day forward, things are going to be different. You can't help what happened in the past, but by the help and grace of God, the past is broken.

There are a lot of people trying to tell us what to do and how to do it, but there are precious few giving us a living demonstration . . . showing us the way. The greatest need in our families is not to hear another sermon preached but to see a sermon lived. Our children are not going to pay more attention to our words than they do our actions. It won't do any good to try to convince them they shouldn't give in to peer pressure and experiment with things that can become addictions if they see us nursing, justifying, and excusing our own bad habits. We'll never convince them to read their Bible and pray if they never see us reading the Bible and praying. We're wasting our breath trying to get them to trust the Lord if they see us trusting our own abilities and trying to figure things out on our own.

We can't convince them it's important to keep commitments if they see us break our word. We can't convince them to work out difficulties if they see us run from problems and avoid making hard decisions. We can't convince them worship in the house of the Lord is important if our attendance is sporadic, no matter what kind of excuses we can give.

To summarize: If you don't want your children to curse, don't use profanity. If you don't want your children to be greedy, let them see your generosity. If you don't want your children to be unkind, show kindness. Oh, I know it's possible to model all the right things and still have your children rebel and go their own way. Doing all the right things does not guarantee our kids will follow the right path. However, the odds are greatly increased when we follow God's will to be godly examples before them. And it's the height of hypocrisy to criticize our kids for doing something they learned by watching us.

Some years ago, I came upon a poem that illustrates this so well. It's written by my favorite author—Anonymous.

A careful man I ought to be,
A little fellow follows me;
I do not dare to go astray
For fear he'll go the self-same way.

I must not madly step aside
Where pleasure's paths are smooth and wide,
And join in lust-filled revelry,
A little fellow follows me.

I cannot once escape his eyes,
Whate'er he sees me do he tries;
Like me, he says he's going to be,
This little chap that follows me.

He thinks that I am good and fine,
Believes in every word of mine;
The base in me he must not see,
This little chap who follows me.

I must remember as I go
Through summer sun and winter snow,
I'm building for the years to be
For a little fellow follows me.

We Need Love

Sometimes we need to be reminded of the obvious. One of the most important things the family can be is a place of refuge—a place of unconditional love, acceptance, and forgiveness. Love is the fuel that keeps our lives going. Love keeps families functioning properly. It energizes and vitalizes a family unit.

If the family is going to be successful, it must be a place where members can refill their empty tanks.

Everybody—mom, dad, brother, sister—needs love. Not the stuff that passes for love in romance novels or fairy-tale movies. Not the "I'll love you if you love me, but when times get hard I'm going to look for something or somebody else" sentiment that passes for love in our world.

The kind of love we need is strong, caring, and secure. It looks for and believes the best. It is committed and faithful even when facing the brunt of life's storms. It seeks the highest good of others. It sacrifices oneself in order to promote the other. It is unrelenting, even when disappointed.

The kind of love that causes families to be successful was modeled by the Lord Jesus.

Selfless Love
In Philippians 2:7, the Bible says Jesus made of Himself *"no reputation."* One translation says He *"emptied Himself "* (NASB). When Jesus loves, it isn't about what's best for HIM; it's about what's best for US. Selfless love.

Serving Love
Instead of *what am I going to get out of it?* The concern is, *what can I do for you?* We see this kind of love in the Upper Room in the Gospel of John, chapter 13. Jesus removed His outer garment, wrapped a towel around His waist, took a basin of water, and washed each of His disciples' feet. Though He was the greatest, He humbled Himself as the least.

Sacrificial Love
Jesus said, *"Greater love has no one than this, that one lay down his life for his friends"* (John 15:13). This sacrificial love was personified by God the Father, who *"so loved the world that He gave His only begotten Son"* (3:16).

This kind of love makes families successful. It is not confined to feelings and attitudes, but involves choices that express discipleship to Jesus. When the Bible talks about sacrificial love in a family, it describes it as *mutual submission* (see Ephesians 5:20). We live in a world that emphasizes equality, but even if you have equality, there is an ongoing battle of rights. Equality can exist without love, but it won't create a Christian community or a successful, godly family. With mutual submission you give up rights and support one another. Mutual submission doesn't allow you to promote yourself and your own interests, but neither does it make you a doormat to be used by others. Legitimate submission cannot be coerced. In the end, submission is humility as expressed in the self-giving, sacrificial love of Jesus.

We Need the Lord

There is a lot of good advice available these days about the family, but the most important dimension for Christians is the spiritual dimension. The most important ingredient is putting Jesus at the center of the home and the head of the family. It begins with surrendering our life to Jesus and embracing His lordship as a core value of the family unit.

We hear all kinds of stereotypes about people based on traits that have been handed down through the generations. There are generalizations based on ethnicity, economics, education, genetics, and many other influences. We say things like, "The apple doesn't fall very far from the tree." These stereotypes become limitations we arbitrarily place on ourselves and others. The good news is that in Jesus, all the barriers are removed.

Maybe your past hasn't been ideal. Maybe what's running through your family tree isn't very positive. What's been handed to you may include heartache, tragedy, and pain. It may contain disappointment and sorrow, abuse and shame, physical challenges, poverty, and disease. What's been passed on to you may include abandonment, loneliness, hatred, distrust, promiscuity, and other negatives too horrible to mention.

If someone were to look at your family tree, they might read only impossibility, dysfunction, and ruin.

The good news is this does not have to be the end of the story. If you are in Jesus—if He is your Lord—there is another side to your family. This is what Paul said in Galatians 3:26-29 (New Life Version):

> You are now children of God because you have put your trust in Christ Jesus. All of you who have been baptized to show you belong to Christ have become like Christ. God does not see you as a Jew or as a Greek. He does not see you as a servant or as a person free to work. He does not see you as a man or as a woman. You are all one in Christ. If you belong to Christ, then you have become the true children of Abraham. What God promised to him is now yours.

Now that Jesus is Lord, we are part of a different family tree than our biological family of origin. We are Abraham's offspring; heirs according to the promise given to him by God.

In the natural, our family heritage may have spelled disaster, defeat, and dysfunction. In the natural, we are powerless to break the perpetuation of those negatives. Now, through the grace of God, we have a new, spiritual heritage. When Jesus is Lord of the family, it makes us distinct from all unbelieving families. It removes all the limitations and sets us on the path to true freedom.

Our new heritage is through Abraham, who was a friend of God. In our family tree is Moses, who spoke face-to-face with God. When Jesus is Lord we not only get a new family history, we also get a new DNA.

Woven into our new DNA is the forgiving spirit of Joseph. A strand in our new DNA gives us the strategic ability of Joshua. There are strands giving us the resolve of Deborah, the devotion of Ruth, the courage of David, the wisdom of Solomon, the leadership ability of Nehemiah, the power of Elijah, the anointing of Elisha, the compassion of Jeremiah, the boldness of Daniel, the determination of Shadrach and Meshach and Abednego, and the confidence of Ezekiel. All of this is now built into our bloodline.

The promise of Jesus is Revelation 21:5: *"Behold, I am making all things new."*

Knowing this is encouraging. It also challenges us to live according to this new family history that is the reward of those who surrender to Jesus.

The challenge is to model servant leadership to our loved ones. To demonstrate that selfless, serving, sacrificial love that seeks what is best for our family members. To surrender to Jesus as Lord of our life and as the centerpiece of our home. To live by the new DNA He has placed within us.

Our world is watching—desperately hoping to find something better than what it has. These qualities of *Leadership, Love,* and *Lord* will cause our families to bear witness of what a family of true disciples is supposed to be. This kind of family is the hope of a world in troubled times like these.

8

Generously Giving

For almost 50 years, my dad pastored small rural congregations in Florida. The ability of most of those churches to pay the pastor a living wage for him and his family was limited, so Dad was bi-vocational. Even though the churches provided a house (parsonage) for our family to live in, resources were scarce. Consequently, when he was no longer able to serve in the pastorate and needed to retire, my father had very little in savings and, most concerning, had no place to live.

One day, out of the blue, Dad received a call from a man he had ministered to years before. Upon learning my dad was ready to retire but had no place to live, the man asked him not to make any decisions until he was able to get back to him. Weeks passed, and when Dad didn't hear anything, he resigned himself to trying to find a way out of the dilemma by himself. Then the man called again asking Dad to come to Arkansas and look at a house.

The house needed some work, but the man said if Dad liked it and would help fix it up, the man would buy it. Then he added, "I will let you live in it for as long as you like. It will not cost you anything but utilities and insurance on your personal property."

With a grateful heart, Dad accepted the man's offer. He lived out his retirement years until his death in that house so generously provided by this faithful servant of the Lord.

I thought of this man and his generous gift to my father when I was reading about the gift the Philippian church sent to the Apostle Paul. Both he and the Philippians illustrated a quality of *generosity* that is characteristic of true followers of Jesus.

The best way to gauge when someone is spiritually maturing isn't to look at how many Bible verses they can quote or how many chapters they read each day. It isn't by measuring the amount of time they spend on their knees in prayer or how often they are in church each week. All of those things are indeed important, but they aren't the primary means the Bible uses to measure the growth of a follower of Jesus.

Instead, there are two questions that help define our spiritual growth. First, how are we serving? Second, how are we giving? Our commitment is found in how much we are serving and giving.

When we look at the life and ministry of Jesus, we discover He talked about giving more than He talked about Heaven and hell combined. Sixteen of the thirty-eight parables Jesus taught were about money or possessions. One out of every ten verses in the Gospels deals with money.

The reason Jesus talks about money so much is because our heart is bound to our wallet. He doesn't want or need our money. He wants our heart, but He knows our heart is attached to our money. That's why He said, *"Where your treasure is, there your heart will be also"* (Matthew 6:21).

Giving isn't God's way of raising funds; it's His way of raising His children. He wants us to love Him with all our heart, and giving is how we learn to do that. We can say we love Jesus, but if we aren't giving to Him in some capacity, our words don't mean much.

Someone has accurately observed, *You can give without loving, but you can't love without giving.*

A tension exists in every person who follows Jesus in this area of generosity. On the one hand, the fantastic rewards for faithful giving prompts people to radically give their money. On the other hand, wise stewardship and care for the future urges people to save their money. The tension is real between how much to keep and how much to give.

When it comes to giving, the New Testament standard is *generosity*. That will mean different things for different people.

It isn't about a certain amount or even a certain percentage. It's about the motivation of the heart. Generosity requires a bigness of heart. It requires an open hand, a compassionate spirit, and an unselfish attitude.

This quality was found in the man who was so generous to my father, and it is illustrated in the Apostle Paul's letter to the church in Philippi.

We are first introduced to the Philippians in Acts 16. Paul went to Philippi along with his traveling companion, Silas, in response to a vision he had of a man from Macedonia calling for him to "come over . . . and help us" (v. 9). A series of dramatic demonstrations of God's power working through Paul and Silas resulted in the establishment of a strong, vibrant, generous church in that city.

For the rest of his ministry, Paul had a special connection with the Philippian church. Regardless of the trials he faced, the Philippian church faithfully invested in the ministry of the man who had introduced them to the Gospel. The last part of the letter he wrote to this church that was dear to his heart was a thank-you note of appreciation for their ongoing support given to his ministry. The specific occasion that prompted the writing of this letter was a generous gift this church had sent to him.

For two years, the church in Philippi had lost touch with Paul. They didn't know where he was after he had been arrested in Jerusalem and then put in prison. The next time they heard about him, he had been transferred to a prison in Rome. Once they knew where he was, they got in touch with him and apologized for not having contact with him and therefore not supporting him during those years. In his letter, Paul rejoiced to see their growth in the Lord (1:3-11). He noted their progress and was aware of their lack of opportunity to express their love and concern (4:10). He commended them for unselfishly focusing on his needs instead of their own (vv. 14-15).

As he closed his letter, Paul thanked them for their generosity. The observations he made about their generosity are true about the generosity of every follower of Jesus.

Expression of Praise

The Philippians praised God because they were able to give. They gave joyfully, thankful for the privilege of giving to the spread of the Gospel through the ministry of Paul. God had blessed them through the ministry of the apostle, so they generously responded in thanks and praise through their giving.

This same sentiment was expressed by the psalmist in Psalm 116:12 when he sang, *"What shall I render to the Lord for all His benefits toward me?"*

When we think about the blessings of God on our life—His faithfulness, His help in times of trouble, His watching over us—there's no way we could pay for them. There's no way we could buy the favor of God, but we can say, "Thank You." We can give generously as a way of showing appreciation. We can't afford salvation, we can't pay for our relationship with Jesus, we can't buy the assurance of a heavenly home; but, we can give a generous gift of gratitude and praise.

Paul had preached the Gospel to the Philippians. He had established them in the faith. Their response was generosity. It was an expression of praise.

Not only was this an expression on the part of the Philippians, but it was also the response of the apostle. Paul wrote, *"But I rejoiced in the Lord greatly, that now at last you have revived your concern for me"* (Philippians 4:10).

Paul was saying, "When I received your check in the mail, I shouted for joy. It wasn't required or expected, but it sure was appreciated." He continued, "Your gift isn't something I had to have to survive. In fact, I know how to manage the meager resources I have in order to make it when times are lean, and I know how to operate in times of prosperity. If things get slack, I'm not going under. If things are good, I'm not going crazy and buy a bunch of stuff I don't need.

"No matter what happens in my personal finances, I'm going to be content. I'm content if I have beans and rice, and I'm content if I have filet mignon. No matter if it's a tent or a five-star hotel; no matter how my bank account fluctuates; I can maintain my composure and live in contentment because Christ strengthens me. At the same time, when I received your offering, it caused me to praise God because He was using *you* to take care of *me*."

This is the effect *our* generosity has. It causes praise to rise in the heart of the recipient. This is what happens when we pay for the meal of the person in the vehicle behind us at the drive-through, and when we give to help the person desperate for relief from the devastation of a natural disaster or a tragic accident. When we make a contribution, either great or small, to someone in need or to a charity or ministry, we become a catalyst for praise to rise in the heart of the one who receives our generous gift.

Extension of Partnership

Whenever we give to support a person in ministry we not only support that person; we also enter into partnership with them and the ministry in which they are engaged. Paul said:

> You yourselves also know, Philippians, that at the first preaching of the gospel, after I left Macedonia, no church shared with me in the matter of giving and receiving but you alone; for even in Thessalonica you sent a gift more than once for my needs (vv. 15-16).

In giving to Paul, this church entered into partnership with him. Verse 14 says they shared in his troubles, and verse 15 says they shared in his successes. Through their giving, the Philippian believers were just as much a part of Paul's ministry as he was. Every time Paul led somebody to Jesus, *they* led somebody to Jesus. When Paul planted a church, *they* planted a church. Paul's ministry was their ministry because of their support.

Not everyone can go. Not everyone can preach or teach. Not everyone can do physical labor on a church or school building. Yet, our generosity makes us a partner with those who are going and preaching and laboring.

Henri Nouwen said:

> Fund-raising is proclaiming what we believe in such a way that we offer other people an opportunity to participate with us in our vision and mission. Fund-raising is precisely the opposite of begging. When we seek to raise funds, we are not saying, "Please, could you help us out because lately it's been hard." Rather, we are declaring, "We have a vision that is amazing and exciting. We are inviting you to invest yourself through the resources that God has given you—your energy, your prayer, and your money—in this work to which God has called us.

Generosity creates a partnership where people and resources are united in a common goal for the glory of God.

Expectation of Profit

Verse 19 is the verse everybody knows and likes to quote: *"And my God will supply all your needs according to His riches in glory in Christ Jesus."*

This is a powerful promise . . . but it isn't a promise for everybody. This is a promise only for generous givers. The Philippian believers had supplied *some* of Paul's needs. Now, Paul told them God would supply *all* of their needs. This kind of generosity defies the natural logic of this world. It requires an exercise of faith.

I'm reminded of the story of an African boy who knocked on the door of the hut occupied by a missionary. Answering it, the missionary saw a boy holding a large fish. The boy said,

"Reverend, you taught us what tithing is, so here: I've brought you my tithe." As the missionary gratefully took the fish, he asked, "If this is your tithe, where are the other nine fish?" The boy beamed and said, "Oh, they're still in the river. I'm going back to catch them now."

In the fall of 2017, I was preaching on the subject of generosity at a conference in Hungary. The overseer for the Church of God in that country, Daniel Kriszt, was serving as my translator. While I was talking about tithing, he became very emotional. It reached a point where he couldn't continue. He had to sit down and have his sister, also an accomplished translator, take his place so I could finish the session. They told me the story after the service.

When they were young, their mother had to provide and care for the two of them as well as their other siblings. Times were hard and resources were severely limited. On many days, they didn't know what they were going to eat. Their mother was a godly, praying woman who believed in being generous and in the principle of tithing even though having so little. While I was teaching and preaching on the subject of tithing, Daniel remembered the commitment of his mother—how she faithfully followed the Lord, and how the Lord always provided for their needs. Daniel told me his mother didn't give tithes on what she *received*. Instead, she paid tithes on what she *needed*, and God always supplied. This is the kind of faith exhibited in generosity. When we give, we should expect God to take care of our needs.

His promise is Luke 6:38: *"Give, and it will be given to you. They will pour into your lap a good measure—pressed down, shaken together, and running over. For by your standard of measure it will be measured to you in return."*

His promise is Psalm 37:25: *"I have been young and now I am old, yet I have not seen the righteous forsaken, or his descendants begging bread."*

His promise is 2 Corinthians 9:8: *"And God is able to make all grace abound to you, so that always having all sufficiency in everything, you may have an abundance for every good deed."*

His promise is 2 Corinthians 9:10-11: *"Now He who supplies seed to the sower and bread for food will supply and multiply your seed for sowing and increase the harvest of your righteousness; you will be enriched in everything for all liberality, which through us is producing thanksgiving to God."*

There have been so many times through the years where I've personally experienced God's miraculous provision. Our first children were twin boys, born two months premature. The younger lived only five days; the older was in the neo-natal intensive care unit for two months. I had no insurance at the time and didn't know how I would begin to pay the astronomical cost. Space is too limited to tell all the details, but God miraculously supplied the need. When we were able to bring my son home from the hospital, the bill was paid in full!

Under the Old Covenant, God gave rules to tell His people how much to give. Now, under the New Covenant, God offers something better. He gives His Spirit and the promise of reward and says, *Do you really need a rule to check off a list? Aren't My promises sufficient to motivate radical generosity?* God's provision may not be opulence, but it will always be sustenance.

Here's how it works with God:

> Lend your boat to Jesus for an afternoon to use as His floating pulpit, and He will return it to you laden with fish. Make your Upper Room available to Him for a single meal, and He will fill it with the Holy Spirit of Pentecost. Place your barley loaves and fish in His hands, and He will not only satisfy your hunger and that of a multitude, but He'll add 12 baskets full of leftovers.

With God, it's always the royal robe and the fattened calf. With Him it is always "exceedingly abundantly, above all that we ask or think" (Ephesians 3:20).

When we give generously to the work of the ministry, we aren't really giving to the church, or to the pastor, or to a missionary. We're giving directly to God. Paul called it *"a sweet-smelling aroma, an acceptable sacrifice, well-pleasing to God"* (Philippians 4:18).

It's as if Jesus himself is walking the aisles with the offering plate, receiving our monetary gift of worship, and laying away our rewards. He comes with His nail-pierced hand and extends the plate. We turn our eyes to Him and say, "How much, Lord? How much should I give?" He will say, "As much as you want. Lay away whatever rewards in Heaven you desire." Generosity never goes unnoticed or unrewarded.

Look again at God's promise to *"supply all your needs according to His riches in glory in Christ Jesus."*

God will supply every need not out of His riches, but "*according to*" those riches! If you are in need and a multimillionaire writes you a check for $100, he's giving to you *out of* his riches. If, however, if he writes you a check for a million dollars, he's giving to you *according to* those riches.

God promises to reward generosity according to His limitless riches in glory. This is our "expectation of profit" as generous givers. When we give to God, He promises He **will** (not maybe, hope so, occasionally, if the conditions are right) supply **all** (not a few, not if you happen to catch Him in a good mood, not if the demands aren't too great or too many) our need. He will supply all our need *according to* His riches in glory in Christ Jesus.

He did it for Paul through the Philippians believers. He did it for my dad through a generous friend. He's done it for me. He'll do it for you.

9

Boldly Witnessing

Most of the people in my circle—family, friends, co-work-ers, colleagues—are coffee drinkers. Because I am not, I am something of a curiosity to them, with some even jokingly questioning my salvation. At least I think they are joking.

My lack of knowledge of all-things coffee became evident when one day last summer my wife casually mentioned how nice it would be to have an espresso machine at home so she could make her own cappuccinos and espressos. Ever on the lookout for something that would make a nice Christmas gift for her, I filed away that tidbit of information in the back of my mind. Around October, not even certain what an espresso or a cappuccino was, I enlisted the assistance of a couple of people, started looking Online for information, and began my search for a suitable machine. All the while being very secretive.

After weeks of searching, I finally landed on what I con-sidered to be the best option and made the purchase. When it arrived in a plain cardboard box, I immediately spirited it away and hid it in a part of the house where my wife rarely goes. Once the tree was up, I chose a day when she was out of the house, brought the gift out of hiding, wrapped it, and then placed it under the tree—the first present placed there last Christmas.

The hardest part wasn't the planning, researching, question-ing others, purchasing, hiding, wrapping, or placing it under the tree. The hardest part was keeping the secret! I so wanted to share the news. I was so proud I had managed to come up with a completely unexpected gift for my wife. Knowing my complete ignorance of anything to do with coffee, this is the last thing she would suspect from me. For about two months leading up to Christmas Day, I was about to burst. On more than one occasion when we would stop at her favorite coffee shop for a cappuccino, I had to almost slap my hand over my mouth to keep from blurting out the secret of what was contained in the box under the tree.

Good news is hard to keep to yourself. When my children were born, I wanted to tell the world. When grandchildren came along, I think I did tell the world. You do know about my grandchildren, don't you? The most spectacular grandchildren who have ever graced this planet!

Without doubt, the greatest news that could ever be told is the news that Jesus saves. I suspect you have a connection with someone who is not yet a follower of Jesus. Be it a relative, co-worker, friend, or neighbor, you know somebody who needs Jesus.

It's also possible that your life is the only "Bible" this person will ever read. Your witness may be what God is looking to use to influence this person to surrender their life to Jesus.

Most of us are easily intimidated by the eternal ramifications of our relationship with an unsaved person. We don't feel equipped to adequately communicate eternal truths. We worry we'll mess it up, and if we do, we'll permanently damage the person and keep them from responding to the invitation of Jesus.

One thing I know about God is He's a lot bigger than any inadequacies we have. He wants the lost person saved even more than we do. He has ways of getting through to this person that are not dependent on our competency. Our responsibility is to do what we know to do, and at the end of the day, to trust Him.

In the New Testament, we find most of the evangelism in the early church was not done by professional clergy. It was accomplished by ordinary people who couldn't keep a secret. They shared their faith wherever they went. My experience has been much of witnessing has less to do with what we say and more to do with how we live. Our attitude and priorities must reflect our citizenship in the kingdom of Heaven.

If you want to be more effective in sharing your faith, making a greater impact on the people God has placed in your circle, there's a story in the Book of Acts you need to study. It reveals principles to help you become bold and effective as a witness.

At the beginning of chapter 8, a man named Saul (who later became the Apostle Paul) is persecuting the newly formed Christian church. As a result of that persecution, a church deacon named Philip leaves Jerusalem and goes to the city of Samaria, where he begins to proclaim the Gospel. A great revival breaks out: miracles are performed, people are healed and delivered, and many people come to faith in Jesus. As a result, there is much rejoicing in the city.

When word reaches the apostles in Jerusalem about the revival that is taking place, they send Peter and John to Samaria. When they arrive, they begin laying hands on people in prayer and many are filled with the Holy Spirit.

Now a curious thing happens. Peter and John return to Jerusalem, and you would think Philip would stay in Samaria, start a church, and become a successful pastor. Instead, an angel of the Lord instructs him, *"Get ready and go south to the road that descends from Jerusalem to Gaza. (This is a desert road)"* (v. 26 NIV).

If I had been Philip, I'm not saying I wouldn't have gone. I'm just saying everybody would know I had gone, for you would see the deep rut marks left by my heels as the Lord dragged me away.

So, here's Philip in the desert, wondering why God has brought him here. Of all places, why here? About that time, he hears a noise, looks up, and sees a retinue coming his way. The appearance of a chariot identifies the central character as a man of importance. Philip later discovers he is the secretary of the treasury from the Ethiopian court of Queen Candace.

As he rides, he is reading aloud (as was the custom in those days) from a portion of the Isaiah scroll.

Philip moves to the side of the road, about to let them pass, when the Holy Spirit tells him to introduce himself and initiate a conversation with this man. Philip obeys, and what transpires becomes a model for what it means to be a bold witness for Jesus.

Sense the Spirit's Prompting

When the angel of the Lord told Philip to go to the desert road, Philip didn't argue. There was no complaint. He didn't question, even though the instruction seemed odd. He also didn't whine about how hot it is in the desert. His only response was obedience. When the Lord spoke again and told him to join himself to the chariot, again there was only obedience.

Boldness in witness begins with a decision of obedience. I've discovered if I will simply be available, God will bring people across my path who are receptive to my message. If I will listen, the Holy Spirit will speak to me. If I will be obedient, God can and will use me.

Obedience to the Great Commission and sensitivity to the prompting of the Spirit unlocks the release of the Spirit and transforms you into a bold witness. Making a difference in the lives of people in your circle begins with being sensitive to the Spirit's prompting and making a decision to be obedient. When God speaks, you listen, and you obey. And understand this: *Delayed obedience is disobedience.*

Seize the Opportunity

When we think of personal soul-winning, we usually think of speaking to people who are much like us. Some of the most effective witnessing is done in that context. However, just because somebody is different than us doesn't mean we can't gain a hearing—and maybe even a response—from them. You will be more comfortable talking with some people than others, but never discount the work of the Spirit in putting seemingly unlikely people together.

The key question has nothing to do with whether you have the same educational background or are in the same economic category. It isn't about having the same skin color, the same speech accent, or the same cultural history. The question is whether they feel you love and respect them. It has to do with you being humble and sensitive to their needs.

The differences between Philip and this Ethiopian were striking. *The Ethiopian was an eunuch.* Not only did that say something about his physical condition, but it also meant, according to the Law of Moses, he would be prohibited from full participation in worship at the Jerusalem Temple. *He wasn't a Jew.* He was a Gentile convert, a proselyte, known as a "God-fearer." *He was a high-ranking official in the palace of Queen Candace*—a man of means and substance—far different from simple Philip. Even with these differences of ethnicity, religious background, and economic and social standing, there was a God-connection.

This was possible because of the way Philip approached him—in humility and meekness, yet with confidence and assurance because he was sensitive and obedient to the prompting of the Holy Spirit. Witnessing is not nearly so much about us as it is about the story we have to proclaim. It's about the Savior who has come to redeem and restore lost humanity. It's the story about how broken people can be made whole again. It is a message of love and grace—recognizing everyone needs God's mercy in order to be acceptable to Him. That's a story with universal appeal!

Start With Their Need

If the Holy Spirit directs you to someone and you respond in obedience to His prompting, you can be certain He has prepared the heart of that person in advance to receive you. Even then, too often we are guilty of answering questions nobody is asking. Chances are very good that the burning question on the mind of your unsaved friend is not the identity of the Anti-Christ or the meaning of the four horsemen of the Apocalypse. She just wants to know where to find help for her pregnant, unmarried daughter. He is looking for a way to manage the stress on his job a little better, or how to escape from the pain he's in from a broken relationship.

When Philip joined himself to the chariot, the first thing he did was ask a question: *"Do you understand what you are reading?"* (v. 30). Then he gave the eunuch an opportunity to ask something. From that point, Philip used the Ethiopian's own interest to build a bridge to the message of the Gospel and the eunuch's need for a Savior.

If you're going to reach people in your circle with the message of Jesus, you're going to have to address the things that interest them. If you walk into a man's house and there are deer heads on the wall and pictures of him holding a large-mouthed bass and you don't know what to talk about, there is a serious disconnect. It has become a cliché, but it still rings true that people don't care how much you know until they know how much you care.

This happens in the context of relationship—doing life together. Very few people surrender their life to Jesus the first time they hear the Gospel. It usually happens over time. It happens as they see the truth of the message lived out before them in an authentic way by someone who genuinely cares. As you get interested in the things that interest them, and as you demonstrate your care for them, their hearts are going to be open to hearing your message.

Speak the Message of Jesus as the Main Point

The Book of Acts records many different sermons and testimonies, and they all point people to Jesus. Oh, they may start by talking about Abraham or Moses in order to build a bridge, but as soon as possible they're talking about Jesus. No matter where they begin the story, before they get to the end, they've taken their hearer to the Cross and the empty tomb.

The Ethiopian was reading from the Old Testament writings of Isaiah. But verse 35 says, *"Then Philip opened his mouth, and beginning from this Scripture he preached Jesus to him."*

We must never forget the only hope for the people of this world isn't found in church affiliation. The only hope for the people in your circle isn't found in your helpful advice, the connections you can make, or your well-structured presentations. The only real hope for lost people is found in a man named Jesus.

Talk about common interests. Develop a relationship around hobbies, work, or family; but never lose sight of the spiritual dimension. Always point to Jesus as the source of hope.

Your friends and family may not even know enough to ask the question, but the greatest need they have is the one expressed by a group of Greeks who came to one of the disciples and said, *"Sir, we want to see Jesus"* (John 12:21).

No matter what other good we may do, if we fail to offer Jesus, then we have failed to give anything worth having. The message we must proclaim without apology and without reservation is the message that Jesus Christ is Lord.

The purpose of every follower of Jesus is to get people to Jesus. The goal of personal soul-winning is to get lost people to Jesus. The greatest need of everyone in this world is also your greatest need—the need for Jesus.

Jesus is the best news ever, and once you have Him, you will find it virtually impossible to keep Him to yourself. You can't keep Him hidden, boxed up, wrapped up, or tucked away. When you are truly His follower, you will find you can't keep Him to yourself. That's okay—Jesus is a secret worth sharing!

10

Expectantly Waiting

Once the initial shock of the pandemic lock-down passed, the question I heard from almost everyone with whom I spoke was, What's next? We saw the pandemic as temporary, or at least we *hoped* it was temporary, and there was a palpable desire for this to be over so we could get back to normal—whatever "normal" really is.

This was not something new. Ever since the events of Genesis 3, humanity has been looking for a way to heal the rift between Creator and creation that came as a result of sin so everything could get back to *normal*. On the heels of Adam and Eve yielding to the temptation of the serpent in Eden, God promised to send Someone who would be able to restore the relationship.

The promise of healing, redemption, and restoration was initially spoken as a rebuke to the serpent in verse 15 when God said, *"I will put enmity between you and the woman, and between your seed and her seed; He shall bruise you on the head, and you shall bruise Him on the heel."*

The promise was expanded in Genesis 49:10 when Jacob (now known as Israel) spoke a prophetic blessing over the tribe of Judah: *"The scepter will not depart from Judah, nor the ruler's staff from his descendants, until the coming of the one to whom it belongs, the one whom all nations will honor"* (NLT).

The promise is expressed in Psalm 132:11: *"The Lord has sworn to David, a truth from which He will not turn back; of the fruit of your body I will set upon your throne."*

The promise was anticipated by the prophet in Isaiah 9:6: *"For a child will be born to us, a son will be given to us; and the government will rest on His shoulders; and His name will be called Wonderful Counselor, Mighty God, Eternal Father, Prince of Peace."*

The promise was further defined in Micah 5:2: *"But you, O Bethlehem Ephrathah, are only a small village among all the people of Judah. Yet a ruler of Israel will come from you, one whose origins are from the distant past"* (NLT).

This is only a small sampling of some sixty major prophecies and over three hundred references to the coming of the Promised One—each promise a thread woven into a tapestry assuring God would send the Messiah, the Anointed One, to give hope and help to His people. In the last book of the Old Testament, we once again find a Messianic promise: *"The Sun of righteousness shall arise with healing in His wings. . . . Behold, I will send you the prophet Elijah before the coming of . . . the Lord"* (Malachi 4:2, 5 NKJV).

It seemed like this was just another piece in the continuing unfolding revelation of the promise that was hastening toward fulfillment. But with that promise from Malachi, the curtain dropped. The people expected the imminent fulfillment of the promise, but for the next four hundred years there was nothing but deafening silence!

That blank page in your Bible between the end of Malachi and the beginning of Matthew? That's four hundred years! Four centuries of no fresh word of promise or revelation from the Lord. Four hundred years when it seemed God had not only forgotten the promise but had also forgotten the very existence of His people. Israel had been given a promise, but now the promise was prolonged beyond all reasonable hope. The longer the promise delayed, the more they began to lose sight of and hope in the promise.

If you have received a promise from the Lord, but you haven't seen any recent developments, what do you do? If you're holding onto a promise that doesn't seem like it will ever come to pass, I have a word of hope and encouragement.

Delay Is Not Denial!

Just because God is silent doesn't mean He is still. While you're waiting, God is working. While you're caught in the crisis of the details and can't see your way out of the emptiness of everyday routine, God is orchestrating the events of your life according to a grand design. While you're lost in the minutia, God is putting together a masterpiece. All the seemingly insignificant things that are happening, all the inconsequential meetings you're having, all the seemingly unimportant people who are coming across your path—they're all pieces of a mosaic God is crafting to fulfill His promise and accomplish His purpose.

All the setbacks. All the delays. All the heartbreaks. All the disappointments. None of that is wasted in the economy of God! The curtain may have come down on act one, but while you're sitting in the audience wondering if the lights are coming back on, God is rearranging the pieces on the stage in preparation for a glorious finale. Don't ever give up on the promise of God!

During the four hundred silent years it seemed God had abandoned His people. They endured one enemy occupation after another. They couldn't see how God was orchestrating the events on the world stage to fulfill His promise to His people.

Time and space don't permit a detailed examination of the rise of the Persian Empire . . . followed by the Greek Empire under Alexander the Great . . . or of the breakup of the Grecian Empire into four separate kingdoms, ruled by four generals from Alexander's army following his untimely death. During those four hundred years, the Hebrew Scriptures were translated into Greek, and Greek became the common language of commerce and communication.

Those four centuries saw the rise of Antiochus Epiphanies with his persecution of the Jews and his desecration of the Temple. In those four hundred years was the Maccabean revolt. There was the ascendancy of Rome to a world power and its eventual domination of the people of God. None of these events took God by surprise, but were foretold by the prophet Daniel. While Israel was longing and hoping and eventually despairing during those many years, God was at work. He used every one of those major powers as a piece of His divine puzzle. He arranged the pieces on the stage of world history in preparation for raising the curtain on the most incredible second act that has ever been conceived. The Bible describes it this way in Galatians 4:4: *"But when the fullness of the time came, God sent forth His Son, born of a woman, born under the Law."*

When it looked like nothing was moving, God was working, but nobody understood what He was doing. After four hundred years, all they heard was a decree to go to their hometown and be registered and pay a tax. They didn't recognize the Roman decree as part of the divine plan to transport a pregnant girl to the very place where prophecy could be fulfilled.

Had they been expecting the promise, there would have been room in the inn. Had they been expecting the promise, there would have been announcements to herald His coming and attendants to assist with His birth. As it was, only a few wise men from the east saw the star—the *sign of His appearance.* Only a handful of shepherds in the Bethlehem fields heard the *sound of His arrival* in the angels' proclamation. Only a few poor peasants were present to *worship the Son with adoration.* They had the promise of His coming, but four hundred years had extinguished the light of hope to the point when He did arrive, it took them completely by surprise. No preparation had been made for the King's arrival.

This is the same danger we face today. The promise of Jesus' return is just as certain as was the promise of His first coming. Somewhere in the midst of figuring out how to navigate in uncertain waters, however, I fear we have lost the anticipation that the next big thing on God's calendar is the return of His Son to this earth.

The promise was given by angels in Acts 1:11:

> "This same Jesus, who has been taken up from you into heaven, will come in just the same way as you have watched Him go into heaven."

The promise was spoken by Jesus in John 14:2-3:

> "In My Father's house are many dwelling places; if it were not so, I would have told you; for I go to prepare a place for you. And if I go and prepare a place for you, I will come again, and receive you to Myself; that where I am, there you may be also."

The promise was affirmed in Hebrews 9:28:

> "So Christ also, having been offered once to bear the sins of many, shall appear a second time for salvation without out reference to sin, to those who eagerly await Him."

The promise of the return of Jesus isn't four hundred years old—it's over two thousand years old! But remember, *Delay is not denial!* The longer the wait, the greater the reward. Because Jesus has not yet returned, some have given in to despair. They don't realize the reason He has not yet returned isn't because He has forgotten or forsaken His promise. Just as the world had to wait for *"the fullness of the time"* before Jesus' first arrival, so He will come again in the fullness of time.

The wait is so that all the pieces can line up properly. The wait is so everything can come together according to His divine plan. The wait is for the fullness of time. While we're waiting, God is working. It's too soon to give up. God will always keep His promise. Sin will be no more. Satan will finally and forever be vanquished. Sorrow will vanish. Pain will cease. Joy will come. Peace will reign. Death will be swallowed up in victory. Jesus **is** coming!

True followers of Jesus are expectantly waiting for His return. While we're waiting, there are some things we must be doing so we will be prepared for His return.

Watch For the Signs of His Appearing

You don't have to be the sharpest knife in the drawer to recognize we live in a world in crisis. We have an *economic* crisis: The "have's" are getting more and the "have not's" are getting less . . . and those in the middle seem to be getting squeezed out of existence.

We have a *political* crisis: Those on the left and those on the right are so polarized that any kind of meaningful dialogue that leads to constructive government has disappeared.

We have a *moral* crisis: Ethics have become situational and relative. We have discarded any absolute standard of right and wrong by which to gauge behavior. Filth is paraded as entertainment and debauchery is celebrated in the streets. We've lost any sense of the sacred and the holy.

We have an *environmental* crisis: The air we breathe and the water we drink are becoming more and more contaminated. It sometimes seems all creation is in rebellion, and mankind and nature are increasingly at odds with one another.

We have a *health* crisis: A mystery virus invaded our world, and nobody knew how to deal with it, and the information we got became so politicized and weaponized to foster particular agendas until we didn't know who or what to believe.

We have a *social* crisis: One group is privileged, and another group is oppressed; and instead of listening to one another and finding common ground we keep talking over and past one another. Instead of coming together, the divide is becoming more and more pronounced. In the midst of this climate of crises, it is easy to miss what's really going on, therefore becoming discouraged and despondent. It would be easy to give way to anxiety and fear. That's when we must remember none of this has taken God by surprise. Just as He inspired

Daniel to tell how kingdoms would rise and fall during the four hundred years before the birth of Jesus, so He has already told us the crises happening in our world today are signs of His appearing.

In Luke 21:10, Jesus said, *"Nation will rise against nation, and kingdom against kingdom."*

We can read this as talking about military conquests and political intrigue being signs of the return of Jesus. When we look a little deeper, however, we see the word translated as "nation" is the word *ethnos,* from which we get the term *ethnicity.* This shows us racial conflicts not only point to needed social-justice reforms; they are also signs of the return of Jesus.

According to Luke 21:11, 25, the increase in natural disasters isn't just about climate change. It's a sign of the return of Jesus. The global shutdown and economic crisis that resulted from a virus wasn't just about a pandemic. It's a sign of Jesus' return.

In verse 26, Jesus said people will faint *"from fear and the expectation of the things which are coming upon the world."* Then He warned, *"Be on guard, so that your hearts will not be weighted down with dissipation and drunkenness and the worries of life, and that day will suddenly come upon you like a trap"* (v. 34).

Does that sound familiar? Do you find yourself feeling like all the things going on right now are too many to deal with and it is wearing you down? The external pressure on people trying to cope amid crisis has brought many to a place where they don't see any way out. Hearts are failing because of the strains and struggles of life. Even the saints are stressed, worn out, and worn down. It's a sign of the return of Jesus. Every time you hear of another outbreak of violence, or another catastrophe of nature, or another political scandal, or another epidemic spreading throughout a nation or the world, don't fall into a tailspin of hopeless despair. Instead, *"When you see these things happening, recognize that the kingdom of God is near"* (v. 31). Jesus is coming! Crisis doesn't mean God has abandoned us, or the world is out of control. It doesn't mean evil will have the final word. It does mean the coming of the Lord is closer than it's ever been!

Hear the instruction of Jesus in Luke 21:28:

> "But when these things begin to take place, straighten up and lift up your heads, because your redemption is drawing near."

Wait For the Sound of His Arrival

In ancient times, when a wedding party would accompany the bridegroom to get his bride for the wedding, a runner would go before the procession, sounding a trumpet and shouting, "Behold, the bridegroom comes!"

When Jesus comes again, there is going to be a distinctive sound. That's what the Apostle Paul said in 1 Corinthians 15:51-52:

> Behold, I tell you a mystery; we will not all sleep, but we will all be changed,in a moment, in the twinkling of an eye, at the last trumpet; for the trumpet will sound, and the dead will be raised imperishable, and we will be changed.

In 1 Thessalonians 4:16-17, Paul wrote:

> For the Lord Himself will descend from heaven with a shout, with the voice of the archangel and with the trumpet of God, and the dead in Christ will rise first, then we who are alive and remain will be caught up together with them in the clouds to meet the Lord in the air, and so we shall always be with the Lord.

Things are moving rapidly toward the climax of the age. I can almost hear the sound of the celestial trumpeter warming up. I feel it won't be much longer until the trumpet will sound, the shout will come forth, and Jesus will split the eastern sky.

This is the time to tune in to the frequency of Heaven. Shut out the distractions of this world. Close your ears to the siren songs of this age that seek to entice you to ignore the things of God and abandon the hope of His promise. Jesus is coming! Wait with expectant anticipation for the sound of His arrival.

Worship the Son with Adoration

At His first coming in Bethlehem, shepherds left their flocks and came to worship the spotless Lamb of glory. Wise men came from afar to offer costly gifts as they bowed before the King of kings.

At His second advent, Philippians 2:10-11 says:

> "every knee will bow . . . and every tongue will confess that Jesus Christ is Lord, to the glory of God the Father."

Revelation 4:10 says:

> "The twenty-four elders will fall down before Him who sits on the throne, and will worship Him who lives forever and ever, and will cast their crowns before the throne."

> "And every created thing which is in heaven and on the earth and under the earth and on the sea, and all things in them, I heard saying, 'To Him who sits on the throne, and to the Lamb, be blessing and honor and glory and dominion forever and ever'" (5:13)

This worship isn't just about singing, lifting hands, clapping, or coming to church with a group of fellow believers. Worship is much more than that. As believers who are expectantly waiting, worship is living our life under the authority of Jesus, the King. Worship is serving, as Jesus taught in a parable in Luke 19:13, wherein a nobleman entrusted his servants with money and said, *"Do business with this until I come back"* (v. 13).

The old King James Version reads, *"Occupy till I come."* The worship Jesus calls for is being faithful until He returns.

In June 2006, various news media ran a story describing how Monty Coles was flying a small, single-engine plane when he discovered a stowaway peeking out at him from the plane's instrument panel—a four-and-a-half-foot long snake. Coles attempted to swat the snake, but it fell to his feet, then darted to the other side of the cockpit.

While maintaining control of the plane with one hand, Coles grabbed the reptile behind its head with the other. He said, "There was no way I was letting that thing go. It coiled all around my arm, and its tail grabbed hold of a lever on the floor and started pulling."

The next step was to radio for emergency-landing clearance. When they asked what the problem was, Coles told them he had "one hand full of snake and the other hand full of plane." They cleared him in. He said, "Nothing in any of the manuals ever described anything like this. But advice given twenty-five years earlier from my flight instructor came to mind: "No matter what happens, fly the plane."

This is the same thing Jesus would say to us today. No matter what happens, fly the plane. We may have to deal with a snake, but we have to keep flying the plane that is our life. We must not let what scares us control us. We must stay on course—stay true to God's purpose for us. No matter what, fly the plane.

At the first coming of Jesus, the people had the promise, but they weren't prepared. When He comes again, will *you* be prepared? If today is the day of His return, are you ready? Are you watching for the signs of His appearing? Are you waiting for the sound of His arrival? Are you worshiping the Son with adoration?

No one was given the exact date and time for the first advent of Jesus. In the same way, no one knows the exact date and time of His return. We have signs to look for and seasons to recognize, but nothing any more specific.

We are told His return is going to happen suddenly. The sounding of the trumpet, the shout of the archangel, the catching away of the redeemed—it's all going to happen faster than we can blink. *"In a moment, in the twinkling of an eye"* is how 1 Corinthians 15:52 (KJV) describes it.

So, if you're waiting for the sound of the trumpet to make everything right between you and the Lord, realize when the trumpet sounds, it will be too late to pray. It will be too late to get forgiveness from your neighbor . . . too late to get bitterness and anger out of your life . . . too late to say no to temptation . . . too late to surrender your life to Jesus.

If there's anything you need to do to prepare for the return of Jesus, now is the time to get ready.